SINGER INSTRUCTIONS
FOR
ART EMBROIDERY AND LACE WORK

edited by   Jules & Kaethe Kliot

With the popular use of the home sewing machine, during the early part of the twentieth century, there came a new awareness of fabric decoration which had previously been relegated to the needle artist. The sewing machine, while to some became the easy way of running hems and stitching seams, to the needle artist it became, very excitingly, a speed needle for continuing exploration of needle and thread ornamentation. This ornamentation was never considered machine work as the sewing machine was simply a new hand sewing tool. Not only could it expedite any project but it permitted working without the eye strain which accomodated needlework since the needle's beginnings.

In 1922 the Singer Sewing Machine Company, printed the first edition of this art embroidery book, sumarizing virtally every technique of hand needlework as it could be performed on this new sewing tool. Not an electronic, automated, zig-zag programable sewing maching but the simplest, straight stitch foot treadle machine without any attachments, the only accessory being a basic embroidery hoop.

As you thumb through this volume, much will appear fantasy as you see a machine interpretation of virtually every form of hand embroidery and lace technique, including needle lace, Battenberg lace, bobbin lace, tatting, macrame, beadwork, wool embroidery and even embroidery on wood. Every project however was a reality, each completed at the Singer laboratories, each a further extension of the spirit of the needleworker.

The reprinting of the title is not intended strictly as a how to guide to the techniques described but as a source of inspiration for the needleworker who has for so long made the distinction between hand and (sewing) machine techniques. On attempting the machine techniques it will soon be obvious that the skills required are far more exacting then that required by the basic needle and thread. In exchange for speed and eye strain, manual skills and dexterity will need to be highly developed.

Once the possibilites are accepted, the sewing machine worker should certainly explore the capabilities of the contemporary machine and the new working materials now available. It should be obvious that the most elementary zig-zag stitch will simplify many of the described techniques. The dissolving stabilizer materials which disolve in water are not even mentioned in this book. Today, this readily available material makes an excellent base for working many of the openwork techniqes.

Some of the techniques explained, such as stitching over needles and Battenberg lace are now well accepted in the sewing machine workers vocabulary. Other techniques will certainly follow as the creative worker explores these new avenues.

MATERIALS: The materials and threads referred to in this book are as originally listed at time of initial publication and are not necessarily currently available. With the wide range of machine embroidery threads available today, availability of materials should should not be a deterrent to exploring any of the techniques described. Linen cutwork material can be used where nainsook is specified; linen or cotton batiste can be used where lawn is specified and cotton tulle should be used where net is specified .

BIBLIOGRAPHY:

For additional information on Sewing Machine lace and embroidery techniques, the following titles are recommended:

THE CREATIVE SEWING MACHINE, Anne Coleman
LANDSCAPE IN EMBROIDERY, Verina Warren
MACHINE EMBROIDERY: LACE AND SEE-THROUGH TECHNIQUES, Moyra McNeill
KALOCSAI GEPHIMZES, Katalin. Step-by-step openwork designs.
HOW TO MAKE NEEDLE LACE ON THE SEWING MACHINE, Gail Kibiger

SUPPLIES:

LACIS, 2982 Adeline St., Berkeley, CA 94703. Books and supplies for all types of lace making, tapes for tape laces and kits. Send $1.00 for complete catalog.

This edition contains the original work of the 1941, 7th edition of the same title.

PUBLICATIONS
2982 Adeline Street, Berkeley, CA 94703

© 1987, LACIS
ISBN 0-916896-24-2

FOREWORD

The needle has been the instrument through which women have, aside from keeping things together, created beauty, and expressed themselves since the time some helpful male made the first bone needle. Undoubtedly, the woman of the Bronze Age found the needle of bronze more to her liking than the antiquated bone needle of the Stone Age, and the woman of today finds the swift machine needle more in keeping with the spirit of her age than the hand needle. With it she can do needlework in tempo with the times. To help women create beautiful things without paying the toll of time and eyesight so often exacted by the more tedious handwork, we have prepared this book of instructions for making famous laces and embroideries on the sewing machine without the use of special attachments of any kind.

CONTENTS

GENERAL RULES

Preparation of the Machine

Operation of the Machine

Correct Posture of the Operator

Embroidery by Electricity

How to Trace Designs

Preparation of the Work

Rules for the Size of Stitches
Rule No. 1, Stitching of Drawn Work
Rule No. 2, Cording

Tensions

Embroidery Work With Heavy Thread

Table of Stitches Per Half Inch
Indicating Threads and Needles most suitable

General Rules

IT is assumed that the reader has a Singer sewing machine and that she knows how to operate it, but in order that she may be in a position to learn how to do embroidery work on the machine it is necessary for her to acquire certain preliminary knowledge which is simple but which is indispensable.

PREPARATION OF THE MACHINE

The machine is made ready for embroidery work simply by removing the presser foot and raising the thumb screw that regulates the stitch which, when moved upwards, throws the feed mechanism out of action as it is not needed for embroidery. Feed cover plate is then placed over the feed dog, selecting the correct feed cover plate for the particular style of machine. The length of the stitch is regulated by the operator by means of the embroidery hoops which should be moved as explained later on.

The tensions are to be regulated so as to obtain a perfect lock stitch on the material according to the thread or silk to be used in following the indications contained in each lesson.

PROPER FUNCTION OF THE MACHINE

In order that the machine be in perfect working condition, it is necessary to clean and oil it carefully every eight days if it is in daily use. To remove the lint and dust that accumulates in the bobbin case it is best to take it apart; this is an easy task and is taught at the Singer Dressmaking Schools.

It is very important to use good oil for lubrication, preferably "Singer" oil which is the best because it is especially prepared for sewing machines.

CORRECT POSTURE

The operator should sit in an easy and correct posture, the body should be kept erect and the head slightly inclined over the work. The arms should be kept well apart, the forearms resting in all their length on the machine.

OPERATION OF THE MACHINE

THE FEET SHOULD REST ON THE TREADLE, THE LEFT FOOT A LITTLE AHEAD OF THE RIGHT FOOT, in order that pressure may be exerted on the treadle with ease. To obtain a slow movement of the machine which in doing embroidery work is an essential feature, the treadle should be pressed lightly first with one foot and then with the other, the movement of the machine being started by a slight touch with the right hand on the balance wheel. THIS WAY OF STARTING THE MA-CHINE BY SLIGHTLY TOUCHING THE BALANCE WHEEL SHOULD ONLY BE FOLLOWED WHEN THE PUPIL IS STUDYING HER FIRST LESSONS, and as she is increasing in proficiency and acquiring a more complete control over the machine she should be able to guide it entirely with her feet, as this is indispensable in many cases of complicated embroidery work when it is necessary that she should have both hands free at all times for the proper handling of the embroidery hoops.

Embroidery Work Done with Electric Machines

AFTER continuous experiments carried on since the year 1889, the problem of developing a motor capable of driving a sewing machine for embroidery work has at last been solved. The Singer motor, generally known as the "B. U." motor, is the successful result of those experiments. This motor is attached to the arm of the machine and does not interfere in any way with the free handling of material; it is affixed to the machine with one screw only. It drives the balance wheel by means of an endless belt running from the motor pulley to the groove in the balance wheel and no adjustment is required to drop the machine into the cabinet table.

The electric current is taken from an ordinary lamp socket and the speed of the machine can be regulated to the highest point of about 800 stitches per minute or it can be slowed down to such a point that the movement of the needle is hardly noticeable. The speed is regulated by means of the foot or knee control, according to the style of machine.

One advantage in the use of the motor for embroidery work is that it is impossible for the machine to run backwards; this feature is extremely important, particularly in doing delicate pieces of embroidery. Furthermore, due to the slow speed which is easily obtained,

it is possible to execute lace work even of the finest mesh. With a little practice, a complete control of the speed by means of the pressure of the foot or knee, as the case may be, will be acquired, thus leaving the hands free for the proper manipulation of the embroidery hoops. The use of the motor also means that a larger amount of work can be done without fatigue. The electric current consumed is practically nil.

HOW TO TRACE DESIGNS

In the execution of embroidery or lace work the use of a pattern or design appropriate to the work which it is intended to make is required. As a general rule, in order to obtain even and perfect work, it is necessary to trace or transfer the design directly on the goods in great detail, using carbon paper only in such cases where it cannot be avoided. NEVER USE INDELIBLE PENCIL.

In placing the goods well stretched on the table or drawing board, care must be taken to have all the threads of the material running parallel and in perfectly straight lines, both horizontal and vertical. This can be done by placing thumb tacks on the upper part of the goods and outside of the design, being careful that the design is well stretched. Tacks are then placed on the sides until the whole material is properly stretched and fastened to the board. The design is placed in position and fastened with two or three tacks so that it does not wrinkle. Between the design and the goods a new sheet of carbon paper of good quality should be inserted, (the best color of carbon paper for white or light color materials is blue), then proceed to outline the design with a stiletto with a fine point but which does not cut, being careful not to press too heavily on the design so as to avoid the possibility of soiling the material.

In placing the material in the hoops great care must be exercised, as it must be placed perfectly with the thread so as not to impair the position of the design. In small pieces of embroidery, the design can be copied after the material has been inserted in the hoops.

For tracing designs on net, velvet, etc., a copy of the design should be made on transparant paper. This paper should be a little stiff, and should be placed over the material, basting it carefully so as to be able to stretch it into hoops and then running a line of stitches around it to hold it in position. If the work is on white goods, the line of stitching should be of the same size of embroidery thread as is to be used on the work, and if in colors the line should be stitched with silk or linen thread of the same color which is to be used in the embroidery. Afterwards the paper should be taken out and the design remain traced on the material. The stitches around the pattern should be about 25 to an inch in order that the paper may be taken out easily.

In handling dark materials the same methods are to be employed but in such cases it is preferable to use white, red or yellow carbon paper.

For transparent fabrics such as organdie, fine linen or others, the procedure is reversed; that is to say, first place the design on the table, over the design place the fabric, being careful to hold the fabric in position and to mark with fine lines the outline of the design. This method is to be recommended because it is easier and more precision and cleanliness are obtained.

There are other kinds of embroidery work for the execution of which it is not always necessary to transfer the design, but simply to trace the outline and then count the stitches or meshes of the pattern, as in the case of the Filet Lace (Lesson No. 15) or by measuring the distances as, for example, in doing Bone Lace (Lesson No. 17), Teneriffe Wheels (Lesson No. 26) and others of similar character for the execution of which it is sufficient to have the pattern before you.

Preparation of the Work

TO prepare the work that you intend to do, an embroidery frame composed of two hoops is required; the smaller one is covered with tape or with narrow strips of white cloth, wrapped diagonally in one or more layers, using as many as the material spite of the lining on the hoops, further precaution should be taken, for example—placing tissue paper or cotton between the hoops. If the material to be embroidered is smaller than the surface of the hoops or if the design comes very near to the edge of the hoop, a

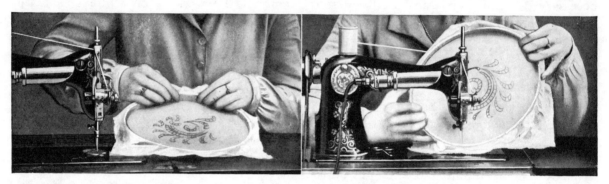

FIGURE 1

FIGURE 2

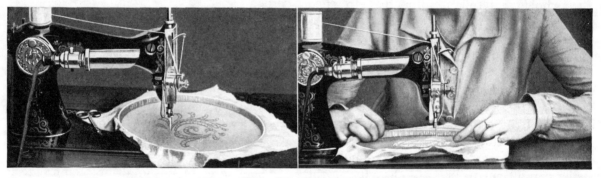

FIGURE 3

FIGURE 4

permits, for it should be well stretched and firmly held between the hoops.

The correct manner to place the material in the hoops is as follows: Stretch it over the larger hoop, then introduce the smaller one and force it in, with the threads of the fabric straight both ways so that it will be uniformly stretched. See Figure 1. Never stretch the material on the bias. If the material is ot such quality that it may be injured in

piece of some other material should be added to permit the proper placing of the material to be embroidered.

To keep the work fresh and not disfigure it with pins, it is advisable to sew to the outer rim of the larger hoop a piece of cloth large enough to permit rolling in it whatever material may project between the frame while the work is being done.

To introduce the hoop into the machine the presser bar lifter should be raised and the middle bar must be at its highest point, thus leaving between the point of needle and the feed cover plate a space sufficiently large for the hoop to enter easily by simply raising it to a vertical position, and then introducing the edge under the hoop as may be seen in Figure 2. It is advisable to always have another set of hoops ready with ordinary material for testing purposes, either in changing the tensions or after the machine has been oiled, in order to make sure that the material to be embroidered will not be spoiled.

After the work is in position, as indicated in Figure 3, before beginning to stitch it is necessary to draw the bobbin thread. To do this, lower the presser bar lifter and, holding the needle thread with the left hand, take a stitch and draw easily the bobbin thread, then hold both threads with the left hand and sew two or three stitches in some place of the material which will be covered afterwards, as these few preliminary stitches should not be visible.

RULES FOR THE SIZE OF STITCHES

In the art of machine embroidery there are several stitches which are appropriate for certain classes of work. Those which should be used in doing colored work, especially in silk, are dealt with in the lessons treating on each class of such embroidery. In working on white goods, all the rules may be grouped into two, which are called Rule No. 1 and Rule No. 2.

RULE No. 1

Applies to all stitches in lace work

This rule is divided into two parts which should invariably be followed in doing stitching on lace work. In the first place, in order to have the needle thread and the bobbin thread united in a perfect twist, the stitching should be done by carrying the hoops before you, that is to say, in the same direction as the feed dog carries the fabric when doing ordinary stitching. In this manner the needle thread twists correctly with that of the bobbin and the two together give the impression of just one thread. If the hoops should be moved in a contrary direction; that is to say, toward the operator, then the needle thread, instead of twisting with that of the bobbin, would become entangled with it and would produce a knot, as is the case of the Chain Stitch, and, in addition to spoiling the good appearance of the work, would make it less solid, because unless the threads are properly twisted together they will not have much resistance.

In the second place, the pupil must follow the directions contained in the Table of Stitches per Half Inch, which is shown on page 12, and which indicates the size of needles and the number of stitches which should be taken per half inch for each one of the combinations of embroidery thread, sewing thread or silk thread. We have shown in the table only those most commonly used in the execution of embroidery and lace work.

If the directions given are not followed and fewer stitches per half inch are taken than directed, the threads will come together, which would be a defect; on the other hand, if more stitches are taken, then the stitching would suffer when taking the fabric from the hoops.

For example, the combination 30 x 40 means that embroidery thread No. 30 should be used in the bobbin and No. 40 in the needle. The needle should be size 11, and 13 stitches should be taken for each half inch.

Another example: Combination 60 x 80 indicates that embroidery thread No. 60 should be used in the bobbin and No. 80 in the needle, which should be size 8, and 19 stitches should be taken for each half inch. In the same manner, one can always determine the number of stitches that should be taken to each half inch in the combination of threads and size of needle.

After completing as much of the embroidery as the hoops will contain, they should be removed from the machine, but before taking them apart the threads should be cut on the back of the material. The work of embroidery on the machine consists in moving the hoops while the needle is not penetrating the material and to have the needle pierce the material at the point desired. As the presser foot has been removed and the feed mechanism is covered with a feed cover plate, it is necessary to use both hands. With the right hand the hoops should be held in such a way as to act as a feed and at the same time the left hand should help in this movement, while the index finger of the left hand, by pressing the goods near the needle, does the work of the presser foot (See Figure No. 4). It will be understood that the motion of the hoops is what regulates the position and the length of the stitches and therefore it is essential to know how to time the movement of the needle with the movement of the hoops. Although this may seem difficult at first, the required proficiency will be acquired after a short period of practice.

RULE No. 2
Is suitable for all work connected with cording

In following this rule, it is necessary to move the hoops from left to right, parallel with the length of the machine, and exercising care to take one stitch only on each side of the filler thread. While doing this, hold the filler thread with the left hand raised about a half inch from the material at right angles with the stitching; in other words, in a straight line with the operator and at a distance of about four inches from the needle. The filler should not be held too taut, so as to prevent wrinkling of the material and the cording become unduly stiff.

This rule is very important, and, under no circumstances, should it be deviated from. The stitches should be made very close together, but, at the same time, taking care that they do not overlap and also seeing that the needle does not pierce the filler thread.

In this way perfect work will be accomplished and the thread will preserve its natural lustre, which gives a very attractive appearance to the cording.

In making a curve, the needle should pierce the material at a depth of only $\frac{1}{12}$ of an inch and at the same time the hoops should be gradually turned so as to properly cover the filler thread, as the design may require. To form an angle, cover the filler up to the point of the angle, then turn the hoops half way in the direction of the other side of the angle, taking three or four stitches to complete the turn, and proceed to cord the other side of the angle. This will require great care during the first lessons and is important because it will be found applicable to the majority of work on white goods.

TENSIONS

Another fundamental point to bear in mind in doing art embroidery, is that of tensions. In each lesson we indicate the most suitable tension for each particular class of work and our directions should be very carefully followed. We emphasize the importance of this point because no piece of work will have the required degree of merit and artistic effect unless the necessary consideration has been given to tensions.

EMBROIDERY WITH HEAVY THREADS

We show in each lesson the exact size of needle to be used, as well as the class and number of thread for the needle and for the bobbin. We suggest that no modification be made to these directions during the course of study, as they are of great importance. Later on, when making pieces of work for her personal use, the pupil may prefer, in some cases, more open lace work or work of more solidity, etc., all of which may be done after the pupil is thoroughly conversant with the proper methods of doing art embroidery. As a general rule and unless special reasons exist, the best results are obtained by using thread as thick as can freely pass through the needle. When the needle and bobbin threads are of different sizes, a certain relation should be maintained between them, as indicated in the lessons. The same condition applies to tensions.

SINGER

INSTRUCTIONS

FOR

ART EMBROIDERY

AND

LACE WORK

FIRST COURSE

OF

STUDY

▼ ▼

SINGER SEWING MACHINE COMPANY

Table of Stitches Per Half Inch
SHOWING
Suitable Threads and Needles

EMBROIDERY THREAD No.		NEEDLE No.		STITCHES PER HALF INCH
BOBBIN	NEEDLE	OLD No.	NEW No.	
16 x	20	$\frac{1}{2}$ –	14	6
20 x	20	$\frac{1}{2}$ –	14	7
20 x	30	$\frac{1}{2}$ –	14	9
30 x	30	$\frac{1}{2}$ –	14	11
30 x	40	B –	11	13
40 x	40	B –	11	14
40 x	60	0 –	9	16
60 x	60	0 –	9	18
60 x	80	00 –	8	19
80 x	80	00 –	8	20
80 x	100	000 –	7	21
100 x	100	000 –	7	23

SEWING THREAD No.		NEEDLE No.		STITCHES PER HALF INCH
		OLD No.	NEW No.	
120 x	120	0 –	9	9
150 x	150	00 –	8	10
200 x	200	00 –	8	11

SEWING SILK No.		NEEDLE No.		STITCHES PER HALF INCH
		OLD No.	NEW No.	
00 x	00	0 –	9	10
000 x	000	0 –	9	11
0000 x	0000	00 –	8	13

The numbers of thread sizes often vary in certain localities. When this is the case, it is necessary for the reader to substitute the corresponding sizes for those mentioned above.

First Stitches

IT is necessary for the pupil to stitch on a piece of material in order that she may acquire proficiency in the handling of the hoops. In this manner she ought to be able to attain perfect control of the stitches so as to take them with the same precision as can be done by the machine itself through the feed mechanism.

The pupil must acquire a habit TO START THE MACHINE WITH THE PRESSURE OF THE FEET ON THE TREADLE AND NOT TO TOUCH THE BALANCE WHEEL WITH THE HAND. These are the first two difficulties which will be encountered by the pupil, but once she has overcome them her apprenticeship will be rendered much easier.

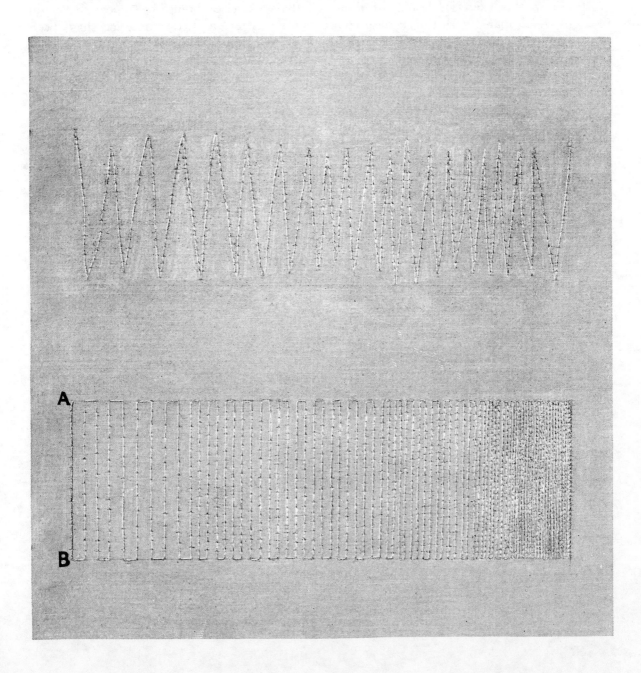

The classes of fabrics required for the practice that this lesson calls for are preferably heavy materials, such as nainsook, which was used in the sample appearing in the photograph, and care must be taken to place the material with the thread running straight and well stretched in the hoops.

The machine is to be threaded as follows: No. 40 Embroidery Thread in the bobbin and No. 60 of the same thread in the needle; needle to be used should be size No. 9; both tensions should be the same as is the case for ordinary stitching, that is to say, moderate and even.

FIRST EXERCISE—The photograph indicates how this exercise should be done. It might be compared with the exercise book of a child learning to write; as it will be noticed that in the beginning there is hesitation and lack of steadiness in the outlines. The necessary steadiness and control in the direction of the hoops and the movement of the machine will be acquired only with constant application.

SECOND EXERCISE—Draw two parallel lines at about one and one-half inches from each other, draw the bobbin thread and make it fast, taking two or three stitches on the upper end ("A"), from this point do ordinary stitching. The length of the stitches best suited to this kind of work is about $\frac{1}{12}$ of an inch, and you should endeavor to maintain the same length of stitch throughout the exercise. When you have reached the point marked "B" lower the needle so that it will pierce the material to a depth of about $\frac{1}{12}$ of an inch, give the hoops one-fourth of a turn and take a stitch on the line indicated to a distance of about $\frac{1}{9}$ of an inch, then lower the needle and give the hoops one-fourth of a turn, as was done before, and you will find the material in the same position as when starting the first line of stitches, except that the starting point will be to the right of the hoops. The second line of stitches should be taken parallel with the first line up to the opposite edge.

This exercise should be repeated several times. After a little practice has been acquired, diminish the length of the stitches on the distance between the rows of stitching until the stitches are very small and the lines very close together. See the photograph at the end opposite to that where the letters "A" and "B" are shown.

MATERIAL: Nainsook
THREADS: In the bobbin, Embroidery No. 40
In the needle, Embroidery No. 60
NEEDLE: No. 9
TENSIONS: Both moderate and even, the same as used for ordinary stitching.

Cording

CORDING consists in covering filling of thread of different classes and sizes by means of very close stitches taken over the filler threads so that the finished work will have the appearance of a cord with a perfectly smooth surface.

This should be practiced every day slowly and with great care at first. After sufficient practice and control of the hoops have been acquired, more speed can be attempted and in time it will be possible to make this cording quite rapidly and perfectly. It is also necessary to be able to start the machine with the pressure of the feet on the treadle, as

it is important to have both hands free in order to properly direct the hoops.

Put in the hoops a piece of material, as for example nainsook, taking care that it is placed with the threads straight and well stretched. Wind the bobbin with Embroidery Thread No. 40, use needle size No. 9 and thread the machine with Embroidery Thread No. 60. The needle thread tension should be moderate and that of the bobbin somewhat tight. Take two strands of darning cotton of about one yard and fasten them on the fabric by means of two or three stitches, then fold them back, and in this manner you will have a filler consisting of four threads. Hold the filler threads between the index finger and the thumb of the left hand at a height of about two-fifths of an inch in a straight line and at a distance of about four inches from the needle. Care should be taken not to hold the filler thread too tightly so as to avoid wrinkles in the material and the cording being too hard.

Begin the cording by taking stitches from left to right and vice versa, moving the hoops parallel with the length of the machine as per instructions given in Rule 2. The stitches should be very close together but should not overlap, and be careful that the needle does not pierce the filler thread, in order to obtain the best results and so that the cord may preserve its natural lustre, all of which enhances the merit of the work.

After the first filler threads have been carefully corded, gradually increase the number of threads in the filling so as to make cording of different thicknesses, then diminish gradually the number of guide threads, (see Figure "A") until cording is made with one thread only.

It is recommended that this cording be made in a straight line until the pupil has acquired a certain degree of control of the movement of the machine and in the handling of the hoops, after which she may proceed to make angles. See Figure "B".

To make angles, cover the thread filler up to the end of the straight line, then turn the hoops sufficiently so as to have material half way in the direction of the last line, take three or four stitches and then complete the turning of the hoops in the direction of the new line and continue cording to the end of the line.

To make curves take four threads and fasten them on the material, then follow them back in the same way as was done for the straight line cording and you will have a filler of eight threads. Whenever it is necessary to turn the hoops so as to follow the design, lower the needle on the inside of the curves. It is necessary to keep on modifying the position of the hoops as you proceed with the curves, since the lines of the design must be followed by moving the hoops and not the filling, the latter must invariably be held in a line straight with the operator.

It is essential for the pupil to acquire the greatest possible perfection in the execution of cording work, as it will be seen in subsequent lessons that it is largely applied in almost all classes of embroidery and lace work.

MATERIAL: Nainsook
THREADS: In the bobbin, Embroidery No. 40
In the needle, Embroidery No. 60
NEEDLE: No. 9
TENSIONS: The upper tension moderate, the bobbin tension somewhat tight.

English or Eyelet Embroidery

ENGLISH embroidery is strong and one of the simplest kinds. It is a great favorite for all kinds of linen goods such as dresser ornaments, table linens, curtains, etc., and is one of the most practical and useful in the home. It can be produced on all kinds of fabrics, from the heaviest to the lightest.

The sample shown in this lesson has been made on heavy linen and has been especially selected for a pupil who has not had much experience. This design is plain, does not offer many complications and lends itself to be easily executed.

Place the material in the hoops with the threads of the material straight and well stretched. If the design is small it can be

traced after the material is in the hoops. If on the other hand, it is a large design, then instructions under the heading "How to Trace Designs" should be followed.

In the bobbin use Embroidery Thread No. 40 and have tension somewhat tight. Use needle No. 9 which should be threaded with Embroidery Thread No. 60. The tension should be moderate.

After inserting the hoops in the machine, begin with an ordinary line of stitching which should be taken over the outline of the leaves and eyelets. Cut the upper thread and after raising the presser bar lifter, draw a thread from the needle long enough to use as a filler and reinforce the line of stitching which has already been taken. To do this, take stitches from right to left, leaving a little space between them, then cut out the material from the interior of the leaf, using a double thread of darning cotton as filler, cord the edge (see "A") and finish the union of stitches in each leaf, taking three or four stitches so as to make it secure.

Bear in mind that in finishing each leaf, the filler thread should be cut as closely as possible to obtain a neat finish.

To make the stems, begin by doing the leaves and continue with the stem by using the same filler thread.

To do the eyelets, if they are large, proceed in the same manner as with the leaves except that the latter are oval instead of round. If the eyelets are small, use a stiletto to perforate the cloth so that they are all of a uniform size as in the design, then cord as has been explained.

In doing this kind of work on silk and cotton crepe or other similar fine fabric, do not forget that after tracing pattern on the material it is necessary to place in the hoops a piece of stiff transparent paper well stretched on the wrong side of the material so as to prevent the delicate material from opening. After the tracing has been finished, remove the paper with care so that the design does not lose its shape.

MATERIAL: Closely woven fabric
THREADS: In bobbin, Embroidery No. 40
          In needle, Embroidery No. 60
          For Cording, Darning Cotton
NEEDLE: No. 9
TENSIONS: Upper tension moderate
          Lower tension a little tight

First Openwork Stitches

IT is advisable to pay much attention to these First Open-work Stitches, for although they may not appear important, later on they will be found of considerable usefulness. After practicing with the stitches shown in the photograph, a better control of the hoops will have been acquired, which is the most important part of the art of machine embroidery, as it is essential to move the hoops forward as explained in Rule No. 1.

The material to be used is nainsook, linen or some other similar material; the one used in the sample shown is nainsook. The bobbin should be threaded with embroidery thread

No. 40 and the needle threaded with embroidery thread No. 60. Use needle size No. 9. Both tensions are to be moderate and even, the same as used for ordinary stitching.

After placing the material in the hoops, outline a square of about $2\frac{1}{2}$ inches. The sides of the square must be straight and run in the same direction as the threads of the material. The four sides of the square are to be divided into six equal parts, a distance of a little less than $\frac{1}{2}$ inch apart. The square and divisions should be outlined with a lead pencil which should be hardly noticeable so as not to smudge the material. This division is made in order that the threads may be equally distant from each other.

Take a line of stitches around the outline of the square, being careful to properly follow the angles. To do this, lower the needle, having it pierce the material about $\frac{1}{12}$ of an inch and then turn the hoops; then draw a strand of thread from the machine, as has been explained in Lesson No. 3, "English or Eyelet Embroidery," and reinforce the line of stitches which have been taken. After this has been done, cut out the material along the left side of the square, in all its length, and also on the upper and lower sides to a distance of a little over $\frac{1}{2}$ inch, thus leaving sufficient space to make the first line of running stitches. Be careful not to cut any of the threads of the reinforcements around the outline.

Fasten the threads, as was explained in Lesson No. 1, "First Stitches," at the edge of the material and in the upper part of the square, at a distance of about $\frac{1}{5}$ of an inch from the left hand corner. Reinforce the edge by taking stitches from right to left, one stitch being taken into the material and the other outside of the material, until the first division of the square is completed, leaving the needle in the material. In order to take the first line of running stitches from one edge to the other, follow instructions given in Rule No. 1; that is to say, after having taken 78 stitches in a straight line, at the rate of 16 stitches per half inch, in accordance with the table, "Combination of Embroidery Thread 40 x 60", you will reach the lower edge and there you will fasten the line of stitches at one point, showing a part

of the line that was drawn with pencil. Then cut another little piece of the material, both in the upper and lower sides, of about $\frac{1}{5}$ of an inch, and turn the hoops at right angles, keeping the needle lowered. Reinforce the edge up to the second division of the square and complete the turn of the hoops, taking a second line of stitches in the same manner as the first, and so on with all the other divisions up to the one before the last. When cutting the material to take the last line of running stitches, remove entirely the material within the square.

This method of cutting the material little by little, as the lines of running stitches are made, is indispensable, so as to avoid the loss of the proper shape of the fabric and should be borne in mind when making any kind of lace work.

After finishing section "A", continue reinforcing the edge up to the point where the first line of stitching in section "B" is made. To cross these lines proceed in the same manner as in section A, but being careful not to pierce the threads of the lines. Then take the other lines of stitches and cut the threads at the ends, after having fastened them securely on the edge of the material.

In order to cross the first diagonal lines, section "C", it is necessary to begin at the right hand side, marked "1", so as to be able to cross them all at once, and in this way not having to cut them until all of the threads have been crossed. Fasten the threads at the point indicated by "1", and then by taking eighteen stitches you will reach "2". After having properly secured the line of stitches taken, continue reinforcing the edge until "3" is reached. Then turn the hoops and take a second line of stitches up to "4", and so on until the crossing of these first diagonal lines has been completed.

For the second series of diagonal lines, section "D", one must begin on the left hand side and cross the lines of stitches in the same manner as has been explained for section "C", except at the same time you will have to make a circular darning stitch at the intersection of the four lines, to do which, take nine stitches up to the point of crossing the first diagonal line, then take nine more stitches and with the ninth stitch join the next crossing of lines and make a circular darning, which is produced by taking one stitch after another in the middle of each of the crossings and as near the center as possible, also with as many turns as the size of the work will require. In the example given, seven turns of darning were made. The number of turns of darning stitches should be the same for all the crossings, so as to have uniform work. When the darning has been finished, take one stitch on the edge of it and from there proceed to the next diagonal crossing, etc.

In finishing the edge, a cording will have to be made, using two strands of darning cotton in the same way as was explained in lesson No. 2, "Cording" except that in this case one stitch is taken in the material and the other outside.

The photographs of sections "A", "B" and "C" are exact reproductions of the three fundamental steps for lace work, which is shown finished in section "D".

MATERIAL: Nainsook
 THREADS: In the bobbin, Embroidery No. 40
          In the needle, Embroidery No. 60
  NEEDLE: Size No. 9
TENSIONS: Both moderate and even, the same as used for ordinary stitching.

Richelieu Embroidery (Cut Work)

THIS is one of the most popular embroideries, due to the ease with which it can be produced. It is largely used in linen work, both heavy and fine materials, and can be produced just as easily on heavy or light materials, providing the appropriate needles and threads are employed.

In the photograph we show a sample which was executed on closely woven linen. Its design is simple and there is sufficient space between the different parts of the pattern, which feature is always desirable when doing this class of embroidery for the first time.

The machine should be prepared by wind-

ing embroidery thread No. 40 in the bobbin and making its tension somewhat tight, using needle No. 9 and thread it with thread of the same class but No. 60. The tension of the needle should be moderate.

The design was traced after the material had been inserted in the hoops. Care should be taken to first trace the outline of the design and then the lines indicating the side divisions "A". These dividing lines should extend about 1/25 of an inch over the lateral lines. In doing large pieces of work, follow the general instructions under the heading "How to Trace Designs."

Insert the hoops in the machine and take a line of stitches around the outline of the pattern but not over the cross bars, and then reinforce by means of a strand of thread taken from the machine.

Begin to cut out the material from the interior of the design to such an extent as will be sufficient to permit the making of the first cross bar. This bar should be done by taking a running line of stitches from "B" to "C", in accordance with table of stitches at the rate of 16 stitches per half inch. Then turn the hoops, take another line of stitches from "C" to "B"; raise the presser bar lifter and carefully draw enough of the needle thread to use as a filler for cording the two lines of stitches which have just been taken. A perfect cording will only be obtained by following instructions under Rule No. 2.

After the first cross bar has been finished, cut out another section of the material up to the line where the next bar is indicated, completing that bar and continuing in the same manner until all have been finished. It is important in doing these cross bars not to deviate from the direction and position shown in the pattern.

When the bars have been made, take two strands of darning cotton and cord all around the design, following the same procedure as in Lesson 3, "English or Eyelet Embroidery".

The thickness of the bars must be in proportion with that of the material and should, invariably, be a little thinner than the cording on the edges. To increase the thickness of the bars, take three, four or more lines of running stitches, or if it is desired to reduce the thickness this can be done by taking one line of stitching only.

After the work has been finished and before removing the material from the hoops, cut the threads with care on the wrong side of the fabric. The pupil should always endeavor to be very careful even in the most minute details, as well as with regard to the work as a whole.

MATERIAL. Closely woven linen
THREAD: In the bobbin, No. 40 Embroidery
            In the needle, No. 60 Embroidery
            For the cording, Darning Cotton.
NEEDLE: Size No. 9
TENSIONS: The upper tension moderate
            The bobbin tension somewhat tight

Hemstitching

HEMSTITCHING is neither embroidery nor lace, it is a kind of work which is made by drawing the threads from the material and on the threads remaining stitches or darning are made to obtain the desired effect. Several countries have various kinds of hemstitch work which are characteristic and at times famous, and their use in all kinds of linen material is so general that it is necessary to become thoroughly conversant with the ways to execute this kind of work.

The first attempts can be made on nainsook or linen fabric, which are the most appropriate, although hemstitching can also be done on any kind of material provided that the threads can be drawn.

In the samples which have been reproduced ordinary linen has been used. Machine is

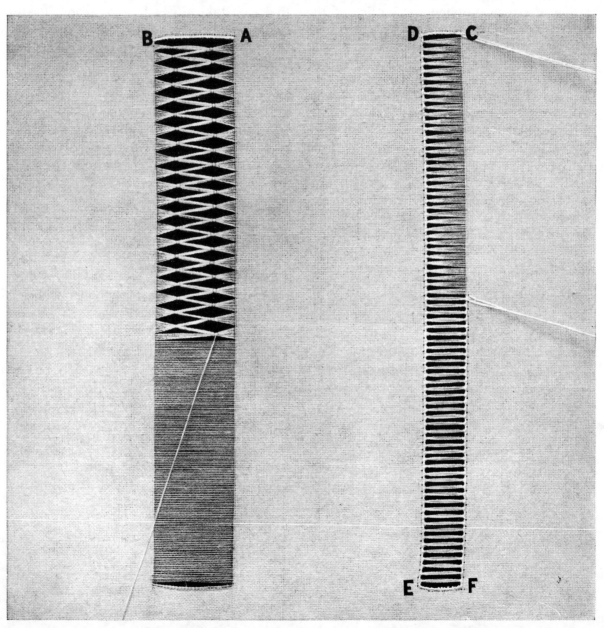

FIGURE 1

prepared with embroidery thread No. 40 in the bobbin and embroidery thread No. 60 in the needle. Needle should be size No. 9, both tensions moderate and even.

To make simple hemstitch or zig-zag, draw one thread from each one of the sides which are going to form the edge in the length of about five and one-half inch by seven-eighth inch wide, cut the material at both ends between these two edges and then draw all the threads from that space that runs lengthwise. Place the material in the hoops, well stretched, and be careful to have the threads straight, then insert the hoops in the machine in such a way that the material from which the threads have been drawn shall be parallel with the length of the machine. In this manner the left hand side of the edge, which is the place on which you must begin, shall be in the needle. (See Figure "1", letter "A").

Take a stitch and draw easily the needle thread so as to raise the bobbin thread, hold both threads between the index finger and thumb of the left hand. These two threads will serve as a filler for cording the edge, until reaching the lower angle (see "B" Figure 1). At that point remove the hoops from the machine, cut threads, leaving a length of about 4 inches and make a knot with the threads on the wrong side of the material so as to obtain more firmness in the work.

Again insert the hoops in the machine so that part of the material where the threads have been drawn is lengthwise on the machine. Now you can begin to tie the threads into groups. Take a sufficient number of threads to make one-half of one group, according to the thickness of the material, and fasten them at a distance of one-seventh of an inch from the upper edge, which in this case is letter "B". Take three or four stitches from right to left and one stitch in the center of these stitches, then make a line of stitches, taking 15 stitches in accordance with the table of stitches, until you reach the opposite edge where the stitches will blend in the material going to a distance of one-seventh of an inch from the lower edge. Then take from the left hand side an entire group of threads and fasten them with four stitches from right to left and one in the middle. Turn the hoops

and continue the line of running stitches. Take the second half of the first group and join it with an equal number of threads from the right hand side, thus forming one group on the opposite edge and proceed in this manner until the whole space has been completed.

For the other kind of hemstitching which is also called first stitch, it is essential to be extremely careful, as that stitch is the basis for all other hemstitching. Adjust the machine the same as was done for the simple hemstitching.

Place the material in the hoops after the threads have been drawn and do a cording along the edge "C-D". Turn the hoops one-fourth of a turn, so that the work may remain in a straight line with the operator, the needle being inside of the material in the space between the edge and the space where the threads have been drawn. Take the first stitch, moving the hoops forward, taking six threads (a greater or smaller number of threads may be taken, according to the thickness of the fabric), then take a second stitch, bringing the hoops towards you and then a third stitch on the edge of the material and opposite the first one, taking two threads from the edge. Finally a fourth stitch in the same place where the first was taken. In this manner you will be in a position to proceed with the next group.

This operation is repeated over the entire length between "D" and "E".

Turn the hoops toward the right, do the cording until you reach the opposite edge ("F") and after turning again toward the right, proceed as you did with the previous edge, taking the threads which have already been separate so as to keep the groups parallel with each other and to preserve the same distance between each.

In any class of hemstitching when taking the threads so as to tie them together, it is essential to begin on the left hand edge, as in this way, when getting to the opposite edge, the threads can be divided exactly. This may be done with the point of a scissors which will be held in the right hand.

In doing darned hemstitching draw the threads from the material, which should preferably be heavy, to the length desired and then place the material into the hoops well stretched so as to have all its threads as nearly in a straight line as possible.

The hemstitching which is seen in the key is 2 inches wide and consequently corner is formed by a square of 2 inches by 2 inches. The machine should be prepared in the same way as was done for the other two hemstitches

Without cutting the threads, form groups as was done in Figure 1 of the first stitch until they are all separated into groups. Begin the work by fastening the groups to form the design. To calculate the size of these groups, the width of each one should be borne in mind, remembering that the width of each one of the groups should never

FIGURE 2

and the tension should be moderate and even.

Draw the thread with the needle and leave both threads sufficiently long so that they may serve to re-enforce from "A" to "E", then continue to "B" and at that point cut the filler thread, being careful to preserve the angle at "E".

be greater than one-third of its length, otherwise the appearance of the work would not be harmonious.

The design that has been reproduced in Figure 2 was made with groups of eight small bunches.

Take a strand of crochet thread and

fold it in the middle in the first eight bunches, separate these bunches ("F") and then reversing the direction in which the two ends of the strand of crochet thread were placed, that is to say, crossing them, tighten the group in the center forming two "V's" joined by the verticals. This strand of thread should be held, but not fastened.

taking three or four stitches backwards and forwards and being careful in doing so not to pierce the crochet thread. Then remove this thread and divide the next eight bunches "G", continue with the running stitch that was suspended temporarily on account of the the knot in "F" and take 19 stitches until reaching "G". Proceed with the same work

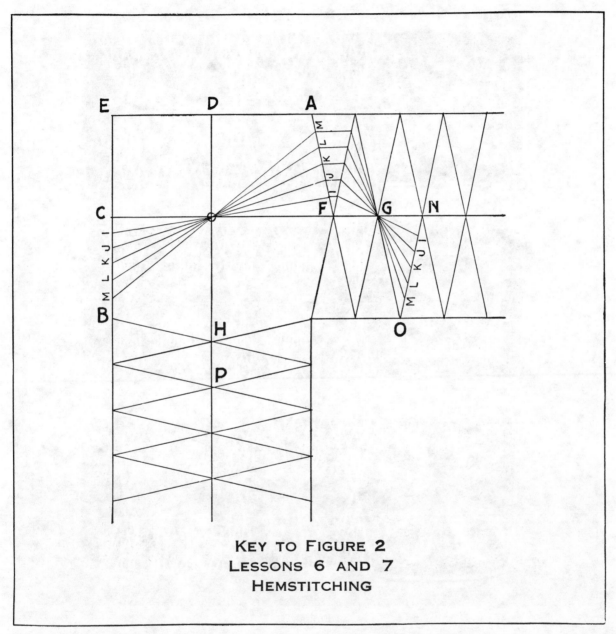

KEY TO FIGURE 2
LESSONS 6 AND 7
HEMSTITCHING

Take a line of running stitches from "C" to "F", taking 72 stitches in accordance with table of stitches, because the space between these two letters is 2⅕ inch, this ⅕ of an inch difference is due to the deviation of the threads when reaching the center of the bunch ("F").

Fasten the group of bunches at "F",

for the whole space of the hoops. When getting to the large group cut the threads, leaving a length of about 4 inches so that they may be carefully tied on the wrong side of the material.

Fasten the threads at "D" and continue up to "H" and "P".

The design which was reproduced in Figure

2 requires, as may be noted from the key, that Section "C" — "B" be divided into five parts at an equal distance from each other, these parts are marked "I", "J", "K", "L" and "M". Sections "F"—"A", "N"—"O" and so on, should be marked in the same manner.

reach the first four bunches which will be fastened with two stitches and a third stitch should be made across the line of running stitches that were made at "I" and section "F"—"A". Take two stitches and tie the other four bunches of the group, then make a line of stitches taking care when passing over "G"

Figure 3

After fastening the threads at "I" of that section which is marked "C"—"B", make a line of running stitches until you reach "I" of section "F"—"A", being careful that the number of stitches is correct, and also that the union of threads "C" to "F" and "D" to "H" is not pierced. Continue until you

not to punch the center. Then follow as far as "I" over section "N"—"O" where the same number of bunches should be fastened together as before.

Continue zig-zagging until the full length of the work to be done has been covered and cut the threads, leaving a length of about 4 inches so as to be able to fasten them properly on the wrong side of the material.

Fasten the threads at "J" over section "C" —"B", making a line of stitches up to "J" in seection "F"—"A". Following section "N"— "O" in "J", observe the same care as when "I" was made. The running stitches "K", "L" and "M" must be crossed as was explained in connection with "I" and "J".

Section "F"—"A" shall be the basis for the pattern of the bunches. In "I" there are two groups of four bunches each, in "J" the groups are of 1, 2, 2, 2, 1, in "K" 2, 2, 2, in "L" 1, 2, 2, 2, 1 and in "M" 2, 2, 2, 2.

The running stitches should never be finished in a place such as "G" but should be finished in section, as for example: "N"—"O", because another thread would have to be added in changing the hoops as this would show a very large spot. After all the running stitches have been made from section "C"—"B" make section "C" —"E", "E"—"D", "D"—"A" and finish the crossing of the threads so as to be in a position to begin the darning stitch.

To make the corner the center must be very carefully prepared. At the point where the threads cross 10 or more stitches should be taken in any direction around the center, or they can also be taken in the form of a cross or spot. Make a darning stitch, going over three times and taking two threads at each stitch. Threads to be taken should alternate, that is, taking every other thread when going over the second and third time, to do this move the hoops with a circular motion. From this point continue darning as shown in the photograph, always taking one stitch only between the threads until the widest part is reached, then gradually release the threads one by one until you get to the narrowest part and according to the shape which you desire to give to the darning. Proceed in the same manner in making the darning stitches at the lower end of the square in the corner. This may be done with any variety of design that you may wish.

In darning always be careful to see that the rows of stitches which form the design are close together to those that were taken previously.

After finishing the darning make a buttonhole stitch between "A", "E" and "B", in that part which was reinforced first. For this purpose you will have to change the tensions, the upper tension shall have to be moderate and the lower tension somewhat tight. Make a line of basting with a piece of darning cotton and draw from the machine a strand of thread twice as long as actually required. This strand of thread should serve as a filler and should be fastened with a stitch at letter "A". This filler should be carried on the interior of the corner, that is, in that part which is over the lace work, and one stitch is to be taken at the edge of the material, another stitch between the edge and the filler and a third stitch over the right hand side of the filler, returning in the same manner but in a reverse direction until you have reached the edge of the material, and so on to the end, always being careful that the stitches are as close to each other as possible (Rule 2). The buttonhole stitch is made on the edge of the material after all other work has been done so as to give it a neat appearance. The filler must be thicker than the edge.

Figure 3 shows three attractive pieces of hemstitching work with darned corners. They were made in the manner which we have explained, the only exception being that the darning design is different. The designs may be changed to suit the individual taste of the operator, always remembering that it is necessary to cross the threads and to group the bunches artistically.

MATERIAL: Ordinary linen
THREADS: In the bobbin, Embroidery No. 40
            In the needle, Embroidery No. 60
            To fasten the bunches of threads
            Crochet Thread
NEEDLE: Size No. 9
TENSIONS: For hemstitching, both moderate and even.
            For buttonhole, the upper tension moderate and the bobbin tension a little tight.

Scalloping and Raised Embroidery
Satin Stitch

THIS is one of the most useful varieties of embroidery as it is used not only on personal wear, but also on bed linen, table linen, etc. The Raised Embroidery, as well as the Scalloping, are made by following Rule 2, but considerable perseverance and practice are required to obtain perfect execution, as it is essential that the separation of the stitches be not noticeable and lengthened or shortened according to the requirements of the design. Both varieties of embroidery can be made either on heavy or light fabrics.

However, when using net, cotton crepe, washable silk or other similar materials, you will have to place on the wrong side of the material, as a reinforcement, a piece of transparent drawing paper so as to give body to the material and prevent fabric from opening. The paper can easily be removed after the work has been finished and there shall

remain only very small pieces covered with the stitches.

The sample shown in the photograph has been made on very heavy material. This sort of material is more easily worked by a beginner.

After the material has been placed in the hoops, well stretched and with the threads true, draw the pattern as has been explained in previous lessons, and then proceed to prepare the machine. Use embroidery thread No. 40 in the bobbin and No. 60 embroidery thread of the same kind in the needle. Needle should be size No. 9. The upper tension should be moderate and the lower tension a little tight.

In doing Raised Embroidery run a line of basting stitches, using darning cotton, around the outline of the leaves, cut the guide at the end as short as possible in order to obtain neatness. Cover the interior of the space with long stitches until the entire space has been filled. See "A". Fasten a new guide of the same cotton at the point of the leaf taking care to preserve the proper proportions of the leaf, and do the raised work following instructions contained in Lesson No. 2 ("Cording").

Begin to embroider slowly and continue in the same manner until sufficient ease and control of the movement of the hoops have been acquired, so as to make certain that the stitches are exactly taken where required.

In doing the stems, first make the leaves that appear detached and then those that are joined to the stem so as to be able to finish them with the same guide thread. In doing the larger spots, baste the outline with a strand of the darning cotton and then do the filling with large stitches, taking these in one direction only and repeating them in the opposite direction. Proceed to do the raised work in the same direction as that of the first stitches taken.

The smaller spots are made by covering them from edge to edge with long stitches and then making the raised work in an opposite direction.

Scalloping is made in the following manner: baste the thread guide, consisting of two strands of darning cotton, around the exterior of the curve, taking stitches from right to left, which should not be very close together, and holding the guide thread in a straight line toward the operator. Then do the same with the second line which should be basted around the outline of the interior of the curve, taking care that both guides are close together at the points where the two circles join so that the angles are correct.

Now do the filling for each scallop separately, basting strands of darning cotton between the guides with stitches slightly disconnected ("B"), increasing the number of strands of basting in the wider portions and decreasing in the narrower portions. When the first scallop has been finished cut the surplus threads of the filling and proceed with the next scallop, and so on until all of them have been completed.

To do the Raised Embroidery use a new guide consisting of two or three strands of darning cotton and embroider in the same manner as has been explained in the preceding paragraphs. When the raised embroidery has been finished, make on the outside of the scallops a cording with two strands of darning cotton. This cording should be as close to the scallop as possible so that the material can be cut out near the edge.

The photograph shows two kinds of scalloping; one in curves and the other in angles. The latter should be executed in the same manner as the former, except that in doing the Raised Embroidery at the angles of the corners and when reaching the points, the stitches should be taken in such a manner that they all start from the same interior points and thoroughly cover the exterior parts, and then continue with the other sides of the angles.

By following these instructions an attractive Raised Embroidery can be produced and the thread will preserve its natural luster which is so appreciated in this particular kind of embroidery.

MATERIAL: A closely woven linen.

THREADS: In the bobbin, No. 40 Embroidery
In the needle, No. 60 Embroidery
For the outlines and the raised embroidery, darning cotton.

NEEDLE: No. 9

TENSIONS: Upper tension moderate, bobbin tension a little tight.

Letters and Monograms

AS may be observed, this lesson deals with a class of work which is very similar to that explained in Lesson 8, ("Scalloping and Raised Embroidery—Satin Stitch"), but it is more difficult to execute, as there are figures that are intertwined and superimposed, nevertheless the practice which has been acquired in the above mentioned lesson will facilitate the making of Letters and Monograms.

The material to be used may be linen, silk, cotton, crepe providing it is light, or any other kind of light weight material. A piece of tracing paper is placed on the wrong side of the material so that the fabric does not open when it is being embroidered. Place the material well stretched with the threads straight into the hoops and trace the design as has been explained in the preceding lessons.

It is essential to trace the Letters and Monograms in great detail, showing all the ornamental parts.

Prepare the machine with embroidery thread No. 40 in the bobbin and tension somewhat tight. Use No. 9 needle which should be threaded with embroidery thread No. 60. The needle tension should be moderate. Take a strand of darning cotton and baste over the outline of the design, being very careful to closely follow the curves and also using great care when cutting and untieing the threads at the points where lines cross each other, so as to preserve the neatness of the design. (See "A"). Use the same kind of cotton for the filling of the space between the two edges; that is to say, the interior of the letters, and increase or decrease the filling according to the size and class of material.

Begin the basting of the filling as may be seen in "B", using two or more strands of darning cotton and taking as few stitches as possible, being careful to space these stitches when placing another strand of thread so that they do not meet.

A perfect placing of the filling stitches is essential, as otherwise it is impossible to obtain the required flexibility of the raised work.

To do the raised work in the letters fasten two or more strands of darning cotton at one end of the letters and take care to keep the filler in a straight line but a little raised from the material and not very taut. Holding the filler in this way proceed with the embroidery, taking stitches from right to left and vice versa very close together but not overlapping.

In the case of letters with ornamentation do the raised work until you reach the ornamentation and stop the work temporarily, then take another strand of cotton, fasten it at the end of the ornamentation so that when making the raised work the stitches are taken in the same direction as that which was already followed, but, of course, taking care to follow the required direction for each section of the design. When getting to the point where the work was suspended, join the filler threads and then continue with the raised embroidery of the letter.

If you find that by using the two threads together the work is too heavy, cut half of each of the threads and continue.

The little forget-me-nots which are at the letter "M" on the left hand side should be made by taking a line of stitching around the outline of the design, then another around the eyelet which should be perforated with a stiletto or the point of a scissors so that they are all of the same size (Lesson 3—"English or Eyelet Embroidery"), then take another line of stitching to reinforce the first.

The petals should be made with very even stitches beginning at the outside, continue until the eyelet has been reached and then return, taking stitches in the same manner. All the stitches should be close together. After the petals have been finished, cord the eyelet in the center, thoroughly covering the line of stitches and the reinforcements that were previously made.

In the preparation of the leaves and spots follow instructions contained in Lesson No. 8, except that even more care, if possible, is to be exercised due to the small size of these leaves.

For letters or small ornamentation the thread of the machine may be used as a filler.

In doing intertwined or superimposed letters such as "A—V", and in order to obtain the necessary neatness, first make the letters or such parts of them as give the impression of having been cut due to the crossing of the other letter. Be careful with the parts that have been cut, so as to leave exactly the necessary space for the crossing. Also the lines that have been cut should be in exact agreement with the rest of the design. (See "C").

The circles around "K—S" are made by cording the line of stitching with two strands of cotton thread, and the ornamental part between the two circles is then made by taking four stitches of the same length in the same place. This will fill in the space between the two circles.

The instructions contained in this lesson apply to samples appearing in the photograph, but may be changed according to the requirements as far as the number of strands and the amount of filling are concerned.

MATERIAL: Linen
THREADS: In the bobbin, Embroidery No. 40
           In the needle, Embroidery No. 60
           For filling, Darning Cotton.
NEEDLE: No. 9
TENSIONS: The upper tension moderate and
           the lower tension a little tight.

Fancy Stitches on White Goods

THESE stitches are simple and attractive; they can be combined with either lace or applique work and used for many purposes, such as pillow cases, bed linen, table linen, etc. They can be made on any kind of material.

The material used in the sample repro-duced was linen. We have chosen a design where the petals and the leaves are large and clearly distinguished. They also are somewhat detached from each other in order that the different kind of stitches may be easily followed.

Place the material in the hoops, being

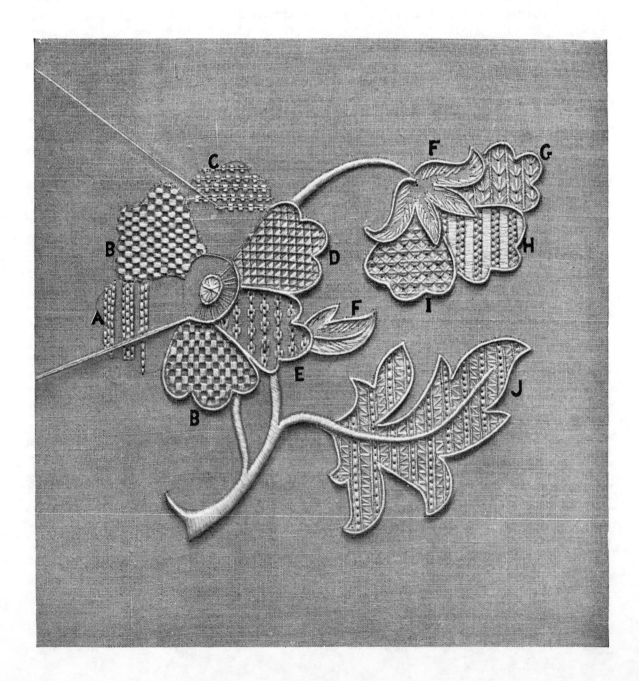

careful to have it well stretched and with the threads straight, and then trace the design and introduce the hoops into the machine which should be prepared with embroidery thread No. 40 in the bobbin and the same class of thread No. 60 in the needle. Needle to be used No. 9. Tension of the needle thread to be moderate and that of the bobbin a little tight.

As a general rule Fancy Stitches must be made by following the direction of the threads of the material, both lengthwise and crosswise, so that they are symmetrical.

To begin with make a line of stitches all around the design.

Point "A"—This is made up of groups of stitches which are taken one on top of the other and should be of equal length and in rows of three. These little groups should be $1/25$ of an inch long and are made by taking five stitches on top of each other. The groups of stitching of each row should alternate with those of the next. The space of the material to be left in blank between the groups of rows should be of the same width as that on which the rows were made.

Point "B"—Take stitches at a distance of $1/12$ of an inch from each other, following the direction of the threads of the material the full length of the design; then take lines of stitches at right angles with the first groups which will result in small squares of equal size. To fill in these small squares draw a strand of thread from the machine, fold it in two and cord the squares alternately. This will produce raised work and will leave an empty square for each one that is filled in. The next row should be made in the same manner, but the filled in squares should correspond to those that were left empty. In this way a checker board effect is obtained.

Point "C"—Divide the petal with stitches taken lengthwise in sections of about ⅛ of an inch. Take a strand of thread from the machine, fold it in two and cord about $1/12$ of an inch of the line of stitches taken, then take four stitches, one on top of the other for a distance of $1/12$ of an inch on either side of the line of stitches. Continue cording and repeat groups of four stitches on both sides of the line.

Point "D"—Take a strand of thread from the needle, and cord in parallel lines about ⅛ of an inch apart in a vertical direction to the width of the leaf. Beginning at the base of the leaf turn the hoops until the cording is in a horizontal direction and draw another strand of thread which should be corded at the same distance, crossing the first lines, so as to form right angles and obtain small squares of equal size. These squares will then be partially filled in by taking stitches, one on top of the other, in a diagonal direction from the corner of each angle and covering one-half of the square. The same operation should be executed in all the squares, but make sure that the verteces of the angles are always on the same line.

Point "E"—This is similar to Point "A" with the exception that this design resembles a chain.

Point "F"—The stitches should be uneven and taken on the bias. These are known as artistic points and should be taken from the edge of the leaf towards the center, that is to say, towards the vein of the leaf.

Point "G"—Divide the petal with lines of stitches at equal distance from each other. In the center of one of these lines, beginning at one of the ends of the leaf, take three stitches of the same length, one on top of the other. From that point take four similar stitches in the shape of a fan which should terminate at the starting point, making a little hole, as can be seen in the photograph. The entire row is made in the same way and then the above mentioned operation is repeated at each center of the other sections.

Finally cord, with stitches on the bias, the lines of stitches that divide the sections.

Point "H"—is made in alternating sections of ¹⁄₁₂ of an inch wide. One section should be embroidered with raised flat stitch. For this purpose both the edges should be basted with a double thread, which can be taken from the machine, then by stitching from right to left the raised effect will be obtained. Skip one section and do the same work in the next, keeping on in this way, doing every other section until the whole petal has been completed. In the sections that have been left blank, make two rows of superimposed stitches as in Point "A".

Point "I"—Take a line of stitches the full length of the petal, repeating this operation twice and taking care to have the three lines close together. Leave a small space and do the same operation all over again, repeating as many times as may be necessary to cover the entire leaf. After the threads have been crossed in one direction, do the same work, but in an opposite direction, in such a way that small squares will be produced. Then take three stitches in a diagonal direction which should start from the center of each square, passing over the crossing of the previous lines of stitches and ending in the center of the next square. This operation should also be made diagonally.

Point "J"—This is a combination of point "A", cording and stitches taken on the bias and in a straight line, all of which form a broken line as may be seen in the photograph.

To make the vein in the leaf and the stem of the leaf, prepare the filling exactly the same as was explained in Lesson No. 9 ("Letters and Monograms"). The raised embroidery is made with stitches on the bias.

After all the points have been made as indicated above, make the center of the flower, the petals of which are marked "A", "B", "C", "D", "E" and "F".

In the center of the flower a rosette was started with long stitches on top of each other, covering half the length of the flower. These long stitches are made starting from the center and reaching only half the area of the rosette. Then stitches should be taken on the bias up to the edge and after they have been finished the two circles should be corded as well as the outlines of the leaves and petals. For this purpose a double guide thread of darning cotton should be used.

We recommend that the photograph be carefully studied as you proceed with the reading of these instructions, as in this way it will be easier to properly learn how to execute the different points described in this lesson.

MATERIAL: Linen.
THREADS: In the bobbin, Embroidery No. 40
In the needle, Embroidery No. 60
For the raised embroidery—Darning Cotton.
NEEDLE: No. 9.
TENSIONS: The upper tension moderate. The bobbin tension a little tight.

Applique on Net

APPLIQUE on Net lends itself to many combinations of work and can be used to advantage in curtains, bed spreads, cushions, etc. It is easy to make this work, as it consists of a combination of cording and raised embroidery.

The material to be used may be organdie, washable silk, cotton crepe or other similar materials.

If the piece of work to be produced is small and can be introduced at one time into the hoops, select the material—for example, organdie—and adjust it over the net, which should be of a small, round mesh. Be careful

to see that the meshes run in the same direction as the threads of the material.

After both the organdie and net have been placed in the hoops, well stretched and with the threads straight, the design is placed under them. This is feasible because these materials are thin and transparent and the design can be easily distinguished. If the piece of work to be made is large or if the materials are not transparent, then trace the design as was explained in General Instructions, "How to Trace Designs".

Prepare the machine with embroidery thread No. 40 in the bobbin and No. 60 in the needle. Use needle No. 9. The upper tension should be moderate and the bobbin tension a little tight.

Take a line of stitches over the outline of the design, and then draw a single thread from the machine and reinforce carefully, When this has been done, proceed with the raised embroidery which appears in the interior of the leaves, following instructions contained in Lesson 8 "Scalloping and Raised Embroidery—Satin Stitch".

After the raised embroidery has been finished, cut out the organdie at the edges of the reinforced line of stitches on the outside of the design. In this manner the net will be left uncovered, as shown in the photograph.

After cutting out the organdie, proceed to finish the work by cording the lines of stitches which were taken around the outlines, to do which two strands of darning cotton will have to be used as explained in Lesson 2 ("Cording").

To prevent the loss of shape it is necessary while proceeding with the work to do first those parts that appear to be underneath, and then cording those sections that appear to be above.

Beautiful combinations can be produced by using silk fabrics with an appropriate net, also by properly combining the silks or threads, according to the colors of the materials.

MATERIAL: Organdie placed over the net.

THREADS: In the bobbin, Embroidery No. 40
In the needle, Embroidery No. 60
For cording—Darning Cotton.

NEEDLE: No. 9.

TENSIONS: The upper tension moderate and the bobbin tension a little tight.

English Lace

BRAID APPLIQUE

A MONG the many varieties of laces this is one of the most popular and pretty and it is adaptable to many kinds of uses, such as table linen, bed spreads, curtains, runners, etc.

To execute a piece of work similar to the one reproduced in the photograph a thin fabric such as organdie should be used which will serve to trace the design and baste the braid. This braid is known as English Lace Braid. There are several widths and qualities, according to the object for which it is desired.

The machine should be prepared with Em-

broidery Thread No. 40 in the bobbin and No. 60 in the needle. Needle should be size No. 9. Both tensions should be somewhat loose and even.

The organdie should be placed in the hoops, well stretched, and with the threads straight. Then the design should be traced in accordance with General Instructions, "How to Trace Designs".

To make the curves or undulated parts draw a thread from one of the edges of the braid. This will give the braid a ruffled effect and the required shape can be given to the braid as the design may call for.

Begin with section "A", basting the braid with long stitches taken in the center, following the line of the design in fastening it at the end with a line of small stitches. This should be done both at the beginning and at the end. Continue with section "B", starting from the center until you reach the corner. At that point turn the braid under, forming a well pronounced point which should be fastened with one stitch. Proceed up to one of the ends of section "A" where you will fasten the edge with reinforced stitches and then continue basting the braid in section "B".

An identical method is to be followed in making section "C" which covers an end of section "B" and another end of section "A". The center should be made in the same manner. To make circle "D" the braid should be ruffled so as to obtain the proper shape before beginning with the basting. The end of the braid should fold under and fasten with basting stitches. In this manner neatness will be obtained. After all the braid has been basted in the spaces included in the hoops, begin with the lace work. To do this, change the tensions, making the upper tension moderate and the bobbin tension a little tight. Then cut out the organdie in the sections where the first open lace work is to be produced.

In the photograph three different styles will be noted.

The first (Point No. 1) runs in a zig-zag line and it is made by making a line of running stitches over the whole of the broken line. Take a strand of thread from the machine,

cord the line of stitches up to the edge of the braid, then turn the hoops and go back, cording the next portion and joining it to the first for a distance of about 1/25 of an inch from the same edge, where they should be separate and then continue to the opposite edge, etc.

The little bars in zig-zag as per the second style (Point No. 2) are made in a manner similar to the simple zig-zag. Afterward make the vertical bar, basting a line over all its length with a strand of thread extracted from the machine. Then make the cording up to the crossing of the bars already completed. At that crossing the circular darning stitch, as indicated in the photograph, will be made.

The third style consists of straight bars (Point No. 3). The bars which start at the eyelet are made at the same time the eyelet is finished. Then take a line of stitches over the outline and draw a strand of thread from the machine so as to reinforce the stitching. Cut out as much material as will be required to make a small bar. Then make the bar as explained in Lesson 5—"Richelieu Embroidery" (Cut Work). All the other bars which started from the eyelet are then made one by one. The material is cut out and the work corded over a double thread taken from the machine.

The rings or large eyelets are made by basting over the outline darning cotton guides which will make both edges. The space between the two edges should be filled by basting three or four strands of the same cotton. Cut out the material from the center of the ring and then make the raised embroidery. This will be done by carrying the thread filler in the manner explained in Lesson 8—"Scalloping and Raised Embroidery—Satin Stitch". The cord which is seen on the outside of the ring is similar to that which is made in scalloping work.

To finish the work, cord the outside of the edge of the braid, carrying a filler of darning cotton, and remove the stitches that were taken in the center when it was basted. In this way all the rough and unfinished edges will disappear.

Where the lace is to be applied to some other material, place the work in the hoops, the lace having already been basted to the material. Reinforce the inner edge of the braid and take out the hoops from the machine so that you may carefully cut the required portions of the material which is under the lace. Introduce the hoops again into the machine and cord the outer edge with a strand of darning cotton.

MATERIAL: Organdie.

BRAID: Appropriate for English Lace.

THREADS: In the bobbin, Embroidery No.40. In the needle, Embroidery No.60. For the filling—Darning Cotton

NEEDLE: No. 9.

TENSIONS: For basting the braid, both somewhat loose and even. For lace work the upper tension moderate and the bobbin tension a little tight.

Brussels Lace

IN this lesson we shall explain how to make Brussels Lace. This is a fine delicate lace of very good taste. It consists of a number of small leaves which are made with braid and lace applied on net. A variety of uses can be given to this class, for example, for altar cloths, underwear, etc.

Trace the design on tissue paper, following directions contained in General Instructions except that no line of stitches is made around the outline of the leaves but simply an oblique direction is given to the stem. Whereas, for the flowers, lines of stitches are made only in their inner circle.

Select the materials to be used, which should be net, lace, leaves and braid, but remember that all these materials must be suitable to the purpose and of fine texture, so that they all will be in keeping with the fineness of the lace desired.

Prepare the machine with Embroidery Thread No. 40 in the bobbin and embroidery thread No. 60 in the needle. Use needle No. 9. The upper tension should be moderate

and the bobbin tension somewhat tight.

Begin with the leaves and the stems. Apply a leaf on the net and fasten it at the upper edge, cording the end so that it will be properly secured. Then move the leaf to one side and make a line of stitches over that which was already taken when tracing the design, taking care that this line reaches the point where the leaf must join the stem. Then continue in the same manner, using great care so that the leaves will be placed in their proper position. Cord a strand of darning cotton, which will serve not only for the leaves, but also for the stems, as has already been explained.

In the execution of the ornamental parts ("A"), take a strand of thread from the flat part of the scalloped lace and draw it until the lace is ruffled on that side. This ruffling must be carefully made so as to maintain evenness and to avoid bunching of ruffles. Fasten to the net with a line of stitches, taken on the flat part. This line of stitches will be covered when the braid is applied.

In the application of the braid proceed in the same manner except that the braid should be fastened at the end and on both edges, then carefully reinforced.

To make the little flowers "B" apply the lace properly ruffled around the circles which were traced for that purpose, and cord them without carrying a filler as indicated in the photograph. In finishing the closing of the flower, a piece of lace will be left over. Cut this surplus, leaving only enough to fold under, and then conclude by taking a stitch at that point.

Now proceed with the larger flowers, as per "C". First apply the interior leaves, then add the braid around the circle, folding it under in the narrower parts. Then do the raised embroidery in the center eyelet, leaving in the center a mesh of the net. After this do the raised embroidery and then the lines of stitches which start from the center of the eyelet.

The flower at "D" is made in a similar manner with the exception that there are more leaves and that instead of a small eyelet in the center, there are five of these eyelets which follow the line of the outer curve.

The lace is completed by making the isolated eyelets which will be seen in the sample and are identical with those explained in letter "C".

MATERIAL: Net.
APPLIQUE: Braids, leaves and scalloped lace.
THREADS: In the bobbin, Embroidery No. 40.
In the needle, Embroidery No. 60.
For the cording—Darning Cotton.
NEEDLE: No. 9.
TENSIONS: The upper tension moderate and the bobbin tension somewhat tight.

Filet Lace

THIS lace is well known and appreciated all over the world. It has many uses for the adornment of the home, as well as for trimming ladies' underwear.

The sample reproduced in the photograph is of actual size and square, but the application of any size and shape can be made by using heavy or fine threads, according to the particular variety of work on which it is to be applied.

The material to be used is organdie, and it should be placed in the hoops with the threads straight and properly stretched. The square should be drawn with lead pencil, making

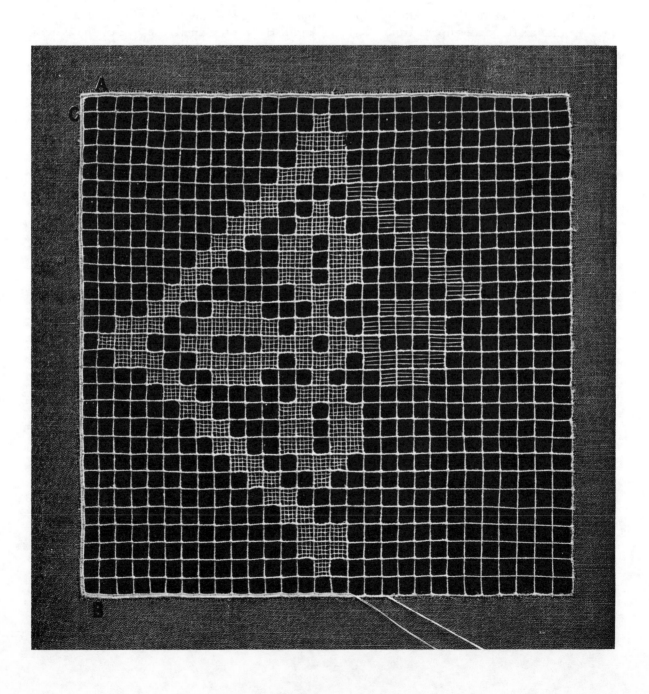

small lines on the outside of the outline, so as to indicate the size to be given to each of the squares in the net. The squares reproduced in the photograph are ⅕ of an inch.

The machine is to be prepared with Embroidery Thread No. 80 and Needle No. 8, both tensions to be moderate and even. Make a line of stitches around the outline of the square, which should be reinforced, carrying a filler of the same thread from the machine. Then change the threads, putting in thread No. 200 both in the bobbin and in the needle.

Cut the material as per instructions in Lesson 4—"First Openwork Stitches"—and cross the first running line of stitches, counting in accordance with the table at the rate of 11 stitches per half inch, then continue with the other lines of stitches until the whole square has been completed. After this cross the lines, taking five stitches from one line to another and being careful not to pierce the lines already made.

Change the thread, both in the needle and bobbin, to No. 80 embroidery thread and tighten bobbin tension a little.

Then cord all the lines of stitches in the same direction as "A—B", carrying thread from the machine as a filler. Then cord from letter "C" to the next line of stitches which has already been corded. Take at this crossing nine stitches forming a little knot and in this way the first square shall be completed. Cord again from this square to the next where you will make another knot, etc., until all the meshes have been finished.

To make the darning, both tensions should be moderate and even. Copy from the model selected, first taking three lines of running stitches in the same direction at each mesh, the lines to be at an equal distance from each other. It is advisable to fasten the extremes of each one of them with two stitches, then cross the lines that run in the other direction, and in this way the mesh will have 16 small squares. When the darning has been done, finish the edge of the square with buttonhole stitch, which is executed inward.

To apply the lace, insert in the hoops the material with the applique already basted in position, then take a line of stitches over the outside edge of the applique. Remove the hoops from the machine and cut out carefully all the material that is underneath the applique, as well as the organdie that was utilized as a foundation. After placing the hoops again into the machine, make the buttonhole stitch inwards and the applique will be properly secured on the material.

The small squares forming the meshes may be of different sizes, but bear in mind that the knot is to be made with more or less stitches in accordance with the size of the mesh and the thickness of the thread. The darning may be of two, three or more running stitches.

MATERIAL: Organdie.

THREADS: For the crossing of the threads No. 200 both in the needle and in the bobbin.

For cording the mesh and darning, in the bobbin Embroidery No. 80 and in the needle Embroidery No. 80.

NEEDLE: No. 8.

TENSIONS: For the stitches and darning, both moderate and even.

For cording the mesh and for the buttonhole stitch, the upper tension should be moderate and the bobbin tension a little tight.

Milan Lace

MILAN lace may be classed among the simplest, most durable and most effective. It is adapted to a great variety of combinations, such as applique for curtains, bed spreads, table cloths, pillow cases, etc.

Organdie should be used as the base. Place the material in the hoops, well stretched with the threads straight, and trace the design with care, as explained in General Instructions.

Prepare the machine with embroidery thread No. 60 in the bobbin, and No. 80 in the needle and use needle No. 8. The upper tension should be moderate and the bobbin tension somewhat tight.

After the hoops have been inserted in the machine take a line of stitching over each one of the lines over which the braid is to be made; also at the corners, and draw a strand of thread from the machine which will be used as a filler to reinforce the lines of stitching made.

To make the darning of the braid, cut out a small piece of the material between both lines of stitches and fasten a double strand of thread from the machine in the center of the space.   Proceed with the darning, taking a stitch in the material very close to the reinforced line of stitches, then cover it.   After that a second stitch to the right, between the edge and the filler, which should be carried exactly in the center, a third stitch covering the filler and which should be placed between the filler and the next edge, and a fourth stitch, covering the reinforced line of stitches and at the same time piercing the material.

To make the curve, omit the stitch of the inner edge of the filler in every two sets of four stitches.

The corners, which have the appearance of having been folded, are made by gradually diminishing the darning at the center of the angle which forms the corner, as will be seen in the photograph.

After the braid has been finished, do the little bars.   Cut the material between both edges of the braid sufficiently to make two bars.   Make a line of running stitches, fastening them with two stitches on each edge. Then draw a double strand of thread from the needle, which will serve as a filler, and cord one-third of the line of stitches made. Release the filler and, having the little bar in the direction of the operator, cross the bar horizontally with a strand of thread which, holding it with both hands, will be corded for a length of about $1/12$ of an inch on each side ("A").   Fasten the stitch at the starting point, cut the filler which is utilized to form a little picot effect very neatly on both ends and then finish the bar with the same filler which was temporarily left aside.

After the above has been completed, make the second bar, taking another line of stitches at a distance of about $1/12$ or $1/11$ of an inch from the previous one and cord it the same way, being very careful to see that the little picots remain in a different position.

To make the circle or eyelet in the center, take a line of stitches around it and reinforce with a filler of one thread taken from the machine.   After finishing the bars, which are connected with the eyelet, cut out the material from the interior and cord the stitches, forming a sort of a buttonhole which, however, should never be made with the regular buttonhole stitch.

Finish the lace by making buttonhole stitch on both edges carrying a double strand of thread from the machine as a filler.

To apply the lace, follow instructions given at the end of Lesson No. 15 ("Filet Lace").

MATERIAL: Organdie.
THREADS: In the bobbin, Embroidery No.60.
In the needle, Embroidery No.80.
NEEDLE: No. 8.
TENSIONS: Upper tension moderate.
Bobbin tension somewhat tight.

Bone Lace—First Applique

THE photograph will convey some idea of the good taste and fineness of this class of lace. However, it can be very easily made and can be used to advantage in innumerable ways, also, it may be combined with other laces and embroideries. The sample repro- duced was made on organdie, which is the material which should be used in making ap- plique lace. Nevertheless, it may also be made directly on the material, whether heavy or light in texture, inasmuch as the material is used only as a base.

The machine is to be prepared with embroidery thread No. 60 both in the bobbin and in the needle. Use needle No. 9.

Both tensions are to be moderate and even for the stitching and the small leaves, and for the double stitching and the buttonhole stitches the bobbin tension should be somewhat tight and the upper tension moderate.

After the material has been placed in the hoops, trace the largest circle, then mark with little lines, running outward, the necessary points to divide the circle into eight equal parts. Take a line of ordinary stitches over the outline, draw a strand of thread from the machine and reinforce. From "A" to "B" cut out the material from the center in a space sufficient to take a line of running stitches. The stitch to be used in this line of stitches should be of a length adapted to the combination and the distance of the threads (consult table of stitches). Return over the same line of running stitches, reinforcing it slightly and when the starting point is reached, cut out the material a little further beyond "C". Reinforce the edge and cut out between "B" and "D" and take a line of running stitches from "C" to "D", returning and reinforcing it as was done before. In this way cut the material as you progress with the work. Take a line of stitches between "E" and "F", then between "G" and "H" and return reinforcing up to "I". From the latter point, continue until the small circle is formed, which should also be reinforced. When this has been completed, proceed in a similar manner with the next circles and with the octagon, as indicated in the photograph.

When the octagon has been completed, do not cut the threads but begin crossing the lines of stitches, making a zig-zag which will serve for the formation of the leaves. Take a line of stitches from the point to where the octagon was completed to point 2 and continue up to point 4, passing through point 3 and so on until reaching the starting point (point 1).

At this point begin to reinforce the zig-zag and after this has been done reinforce the opposite zig-zag and finish by reinforcing the diagonal line "G"—"H", which was left unfinished at point 1.

Now continue with the leaves. These should be made one after the other in the same way as the stitches were made. For this purpose take a strand of darning cotton which will serve as a filler and which should be long enough to take all the leaves of both zig-zag lines. Fasten the center of the strand with several stitches at point 2, thus making two strands. Join these strands and cord them with a line of stitching at a distance of about $1/25$ of an inch. Then separate the strands and with one on each side of the line of stitching make the darning. Take one stitch between each one of the three threads and gradually separate them until the center of the leaf is reached, that is, the widest part, and continue in the same manner gradually decreasing the distance between the threads until they are close together, as in the upper part.

In making the darning, care must be taken not to pierce the threads and also to see that the stitches are very close together.

At the beginning and at the end of the leaf, the extreme ends must be corded for about $1/25$ to $1/20$ of an inch, according to the size, so as to permit the double stitching to be properly placed.

The small leaves which appear in the two inner circles are made in combination with the double stitching. Fasten the threads of the machine at "A", leaving two strands of thread long enough, then draw a double strand of thread from the needle and carry the four threads as a filler to make the double stitch, with or without loops as the design may require.

The double stitch is made by taking three stitches, the first to the left of the stitching and the second to the right; that is to say, between the stitching and the thread, and the third to the right of the thread. Proceed in a contrary direction and continue until the bar has been completed.

When the bars have loops, proceed in the same manner as far as half the length of the bar, then cord the thread about $1/5$ of an inch, holding it in the center. With scissors or a crochet needle, fold in and join the ends with a stitch taken in the same place where double stitch was suspended and then continue with the double stitch.

When reaching point 5, divide the filler, carrying two strands on each side of the line of stitching, which line will be the vein of the leaf. The darning is made in the same manner as that of the large leaves.

The little bars are made in the same way. Then proceed with the buttonhole stitch in the circles and in the octagon and finish with the buttonhole stitch in the outer circle. To do this it will first be necessary to baste on a strand of darning cotton around the outline.

When making the double stitch, it will be necessary to take into consideration the class of material which is to be used for the lace, also the size of the little bars must vary in accordance with the texture of the material. When heavier bars are necessary, increase the number of threads to be used as a filler and make the necessary stitches so as to obtain the required thickness. This is the difference between the double stitch and the buttonhole stitch, which may also be used in place of the former, if so desired.

For the application of lace, follow the method explained in Lesson No. 15—"Filet Lace".

MATERIAL: Organdie.

THREADS: No. 60 Embroidery, both in needle and bobbin.
Darning cotton for guides.

NEEDLE: No. 9.

TENSIONS; For the stitches and the leaves, both should be moderate and even For the double stitches and the buttonhole stitch, the upper tension moderate and the bobbin tension somewhat tight.

Embroidery on Net

THE photograph shows embroidery on net, containing a variety of points. These are a few of the many points which can be made on net or other kinds of lace.

For the reproduction of the design as shown in the photograph, net with a small, round mesh is to be used.

In the first place, the net should be inserted in the hoops, taking care to have it with the threads straight and to avoid the necessity of stretching it, after it has been placed in position.

Trace the design on transparent paper, which is to be placed on the net following the lines of the mesh. After this has been

done, take a line of stitches over the outline, then carefully remove the paper and proceed to reinforce the line of stitches. For this purpose draw a thread from the machine and use it as a guide. For large pieces of work, the design will have to be traced in accordance with the method described in General Instructions—"How to Trace Designs", and inserting in the hoops strips of tissue paper instead of tape, so as to avoid damaging the net.

The machine is to be prepared with embroidery thread No. 40 in the bobbin, embroidery thread No. 60 in the needle and needle No. 9. Both tensions should be moderate and even.

As a general rule, the stitches taken on the net should be in the direction of the threads of the mesh, in order to produce the neatest work. See photograph.

When the points require running stitches, these must be taken inside the meshes and following the direction of the row of meshes, always carrying the hoops forward.

Point "A"—Close one section, taking three or four stitches, one on top of the other, which will have the appearance of a speck, and repeat until the entire row has been completed. In the next row take four running stitches very close together, so as to leave no space between them. Continue alternating in this manner until the whole section has been completed.

Point "B"—Take as a base two rows of meshes and cord one thread of each mesh toward the right and the other toward the left, in a zig-zag, leaving no thread of the mesh in between. Skip two rows and proceed with the other two until the whole space of the petal has been made.

Point "C"—To make the tiny buttonholes, cord the outline of one mesh and then the thread of the next. In the next, cord the outline and so on until the entire row has been finished. Skip one row and cover the next two with two running stitches at each row and so on until the petal bas heen entirely covered.

Point "D"—Cord one mesh in the shape of a circle. Then cord one by one all the threads of the in terior of the meshes which surround the one corded, being careful that the distance between them are the same. The result will be a small star. Repeat this at your discretion over the entire space of the petal.

Point "E"—Consists of small flowers and a line dividing them. Begin the flower by cording one mesh and continue with the next six meshes surrounding it. To make the dividing line, reinforce by closing an entire row of meshes parallel with the small flowers.

Point "F"—Reinforce one row of meshes in a vertical direction, leaving no space in between. Repeat same, working in an opposite direction so as to form small squares.

Point "G"—This is made by reinforcing one by one all the threads in each row of meshes.

Point "H"—Is made in two rows of meshes. Close one mesh on the right, giving it the appearance of a small spot. Then continue in a zig-zag by closing another one on the left and leaving, between each spot, one thread of the mesh without working. Afterwards skip one row and at the next take two lines of running stitches, side by side with each other. Continue in this manner until the petal has been completed.

Point "I"—Take two lines of running stitches over one row of meshes. Skip one row and then at right angles do the same. This will make small squares having a mesh in the center.

Point "J"—This consists of simple stitches and is used, as a rule, for the stems. Any desired shape can be made.

After the flower has been completed, change the tensions, making the upper tension moderate and the bobbin tension a little tight, and cord the outline with a double strand of darning cotton. When reaching the parts where there is raised embroidery, place a piece of transparent paper on the wrong side of the net and make the raised embroidery, following instructions contained in Lesson No. 8—"Scalloping and Raised Embroidery". Do not forget that to obtain good results, the filling must be gradually increased or decreased, as the design may require. Finally remove the paper, leaving no trace of same.

MATERIAL: Net with a round, small mesh.
THREADS: In the bobbin, Embroidery No.40.
In the needle, Embroidery No.60.
For the raised embroidery and cording, darning cotton.
NEEDLE: No. 9.

TENSIONS: For the points of the net, both moderate and even.
For the raised embroidery and cording, the upper tension moderate and the bobbin tension a little tight.

Needle Point Lace and Venetian Richelieu Lace

NEEDLE point lace lends itself to attractive application on underwear, bed linen, table cloths, curtains, cushions, etc. It can be made on many different kinds of material provided the weave permits counting the threads and handling them. The sample shown in the photograph was made on organdie.

Prepare the machine with embroidery thread No. 60 in the bobbin, No. 80 in the needle and needle No. 8. Both tensions are to be moderate and even.

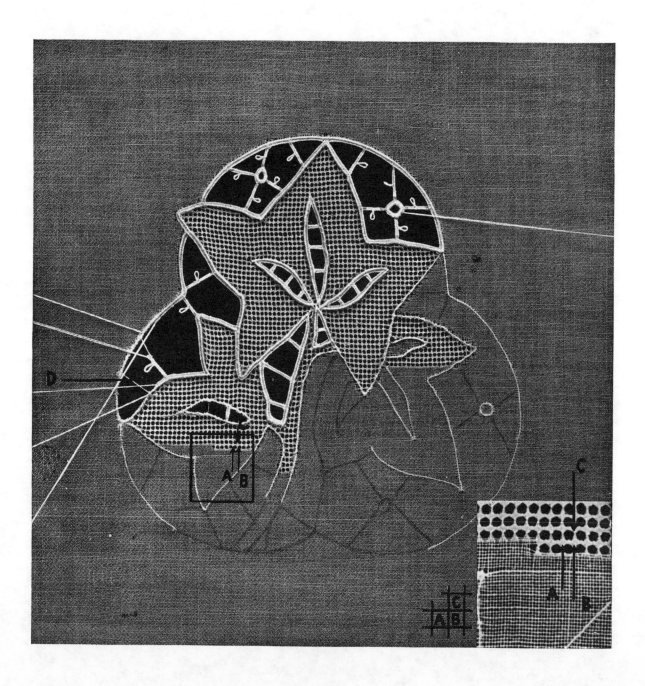

NEEDLE POINT LACE AND VENETIAN RICHELIEU LACE

After placing the material in the hoops, trace the design with great care, bearing in mind the explanation given in General Instructions—"How to Trace Designs".

Make a line of stitches over the outline and draw a strand of thread from the machine to reinforce it. Then change the needle, replacing same with needle No. 19. Begin at the upper end on the left hand side of the leaf, fastening the thread with two stitches. Then take another stitch, taking four threads of the material toward the right, that is to say, in a horizontal line. From this point return to the previous point, taking a stitch which will be repeated on the second stitch already taken. From there, always taking four threads, take one stitch upwards on the edge, that is, in a vertical direction, and then take a last stitch in the same place where the second stitch was taken.

It will be noticed that in order to form the first lace point five stitches have been taken, excluding the first one, viz:

1st from "A" _____to_____ "B"
2nd " "B" _____to_____ "A"
3rd " "A" ___ again to_____ "B"
4th " "B" _____to_____ "C"
5th " "C" _____to_____ "B"

In this way the lace has been started. Repeat until the first row has been completed. When reaching the outline of the leaf, take the last stitch piercing the stitching and reinforcement at the edge. To make the next row, start from the edge on the right hand side toward the left, taking four threads of the material downward, and make the same combination of stitches, continuing in the same manner until the entire leaf has been covered.

The section which appears in the lower right hand corner of the photograph is an enlarged reproduction of the red sqaure in the design and will give an exact idea as to how the work is produced.

Many different combinations may be made by changing the number of threads, in addition to the one which has been explained and which consists of four and four. Beautiful effects will also be obtained with combinations of three and three, five and five, six and six, seven and seven, etc., provided they are made with equal numbers of threads in both directions.

They may be also made on heavy fabrics, but in this case threads and needles have to be used that are suitable to the particular work.

This class of work must always be made and finished in the same horizontal direction in which it was begun, even though the design may change. That is to say, never begin another leaf in a contrary direction.

A variation from the Needle Point Lace is that known as "Turkish Point", which is largely used in linen goods, both in the application of lace and in small lace point, similar to hemstitching. Use needle No. 19 and threads to match the material. Carry a single thread from the machine as a filler and take stitches in a zig-zag line on both sides of the line of stitches, so as to form small hemstitch points, each one of them having five stitches.

VENETIAN RICHELIEU LACE

Venetian Richelieu Lace is generally used in combination with the Needle Point Lace as may be seen in the photograph, although it can also be used by itself.

Replace Needle No. 8, use the same threads and tighten the bobbin tension a little. Cut out the material in the interior of the outline near the stitching and on the outside of the edge of the leaves ("D"), leaving a free space between both. This space should not be larger than necessary to make a small bar. Cut the material in the same way for each bar, take a line of running stitches between both edges of this space, being careful to take the necessary number of stitches in accordance with Table of Stitches. Fasten the line of stitches at the edge with two or three stitches and return over the same line,

NEEDLE POINT LACE AND VENETIAN RICHELIEU LACE

slightly reinforcing it, then draw a double strand of thread from the needle which will serve as a filling to make the buttonhole stitch.

To make this lace turn the hoops half way and fasten the filler with two stitches on the right line of stitches already taken, begin the buttonhole stitch and continue until half of the bar has been made. From that point make a little loop as explained in Lesson No. 17—"Bone Lace—First Applique"—and continue until the end. This little bar is made to harmonize with the material used. But one must bear in mind that in working on heavier materials, the thickness of the bar should be increased in proportion. This is obtained by taking two or more lines of running stitches and carrying the same filler. When the spaces in the background are small, the bars may be made with a double stitch.

Also bear in mind that all the bars must be of the same variety, either a buttonhole stitch or a double stitch. To make the little buttonhole take a line of stitches, carrying a filler of one thread from the machine and reinforcing it. Then in the first place make four small bars around it, cut out the material and again reinforce with a strand of thread from the needle. Continue with the same filler, finishing by making a buttonhole stitch. After the bars have been completed, baste a strand of darning cotton over the outlines and finish with a buttonhole stitch on the sides where the material has been cut out.

To place the applique follow the same method explained at the end of Lesson No. 15 "Filet Lace".

MATERIAL: Organdie.

THREADS; In the bobbin, Embroidery No.60.
In the needle, Embroidery No.80.
For the outlines—Darning Cotton.

NEEDLE: No. 19 for the Needle Point Lace.
No. 8 for the outlines and for Venetian Richelieu Lace.

TENSIONS: For the Needle Point Lace both moderate and even.
For the Venetian Richelieu the upper tension moderate and the bobbin tension somewhat tight.

Smyrna Embroidery

THIS embroidery, as many others which at first sight appear very complicated, is nevertheless easy to make. It is used to great advantage in upholstery work and can be utilized in the production of beautiful pieces of work, as for example fringes, piano covers, screens, lap robes and cushions.

It is also adaptable to ornamental work in wearing apparel.

Any kind of material may be used, for example—satin, cloth, canvas, etc., according to the purpose for which the work is intended.

The sample reproduced in the photograph was made on woolen cloth.

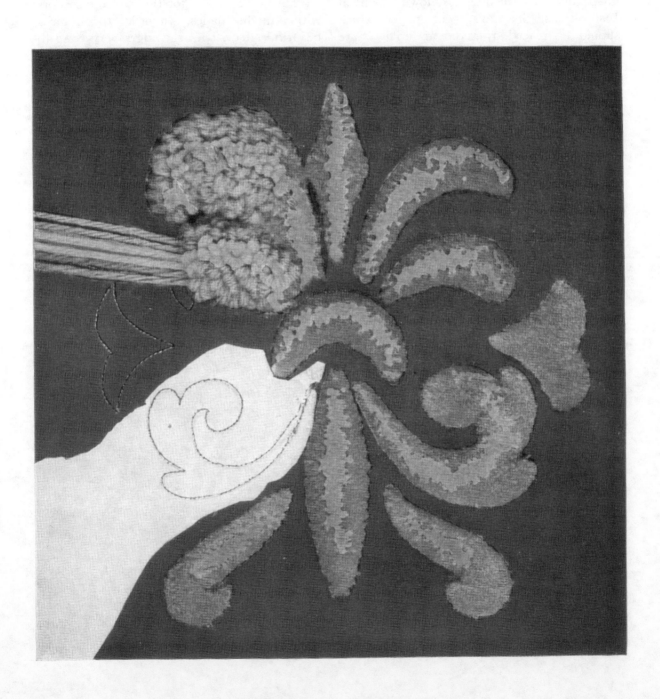

Machine is to be prepared with Embroidery Thread No. 40 in the bobbin and in the needle Silk Thread No. 00 of the same color as the wool which is to be used. Needle No. 9. Tensions both somewhat tight and even.

As the work is raised, it is necessary to lift the presser bar lifter a little so as to be able to move the hoops easily. Loosen the face plate screw and remove the face plate, lower the presser bar lifter and loosen the adjusting screw. After raising the bar, tighten the screw again and replace the face plate. The machine will now be ready.

Place the material, well stretched, into hoops and trace the design, following General Instructions, on transparent paper which should be placed over the material. Care should be taken to have the material placed with the threads straight. Then take a line of stitching over the outline of the design. Remove the paper and begin at the narrowest part of one of the sections of the design. Take three or more strands of wool, according to the required width, fasten them, take a few stitches at the end and raise them sufficiently high to permit placing under them a crochet needle in a horizontal position. Raise the crochet needle a little in carrying it before you, taking two lines of stitches over all of the strands of wool.

Take out the crochet needle and repeat the operation until one section is entirely covered, increasing the strands of wool as the outline of the design becomes wider and decreasing when it becomes narrower. If a shading of several colors is desired proceed in the same manner as indicated, except that strands of wool of the required colors will have to be added.

When one section has been finished, cut the loops which have been formed with the crochet needle, using for this purpose scissors with straight blades. In order to obtain a beautiful effect, trim the edges very close to the material and round out the center.

MATERIAL: Woolen Cloth.
THREADS: In the needle, silk thread No. 00 of the same color as the wool. In the bobbin, embroidery thread No. 40. For the shading, Knitting Wool.
NEEDLE: No. 9.
TENSIONS: Both somewhat tight and even.

Venetian Lace—First Stitches

THIS lace is one of the best known and most generally used. It is useful for many combinations of work, particularly on table linen, curtains, white goods, etc.

Organdie is the best kind of material for this embroidery.

Place the material, well stretched, into hoops, insert the design under the material and trace directly on the material.

The machine should be prepared with Em-broidery Thread No. 80 in the bobbin. The bobbin tension should be a little tight. In the needle use thread of the same kind and number with moderate tension. Needle No. 8.

Take a line of stitches all over the outline of the star in both circles, also in the inner circle and draw a strand of thread from the machine, to be used as a filler. Reinforce the lines of stitches. Four different points will be observed in the photograph.

Point "A"—This is called Venetian Half Stitch and is used in the majority of cases in making combinations of points. Cut out a small piece of material from the interior of one of the points of the star and begin at the widest part, then continue cutting out material as you proceed, so as to keep the material from losing its shape. Draw from the needle a strand of thread to be used as a filler. Cord the filler with two stitches in a space of $1/25$ of an inch, take one stitch at the edge of the material and return over the same line, cording it with two more stitches. This will form a small bar. Make another bar and continue with the others until you have reached the opposite edge, finishing a row. Reinforce the edge, turn the hoops around and make another row, each small bar remaining between the two of the previous. Continue until all the space has been finished.

Point "B"—This consists of tiny squares made with stitches very close together. Cord $1/25$ of an inch of the filler, leaving equal space between it and the edge. Then take three buttonhole stitches as many times as it may be necessary to fill in $1/25$ of an inch and proceed with cording and filling, always taking the same number of stitches so as to preserve evenness in the work, both in the empty and in the filled-in spaces. The second row is a repetition of the first, except that the empty sections are opposite to those that have been filled in and in this way a checker board effect is obtained.

Point "C"—This point is made with small triangles. Cord for $1/25$ of an inch, take one stitch at the edge and return cording with two stitches, making a sort of a bar, thus forming one side of the triangle. Cord the filler with three stitches to form the base, make another little bar, joining it at the edge with the previous one and in this way the first complete triangle will be made. Cord the filler with two stitches, make another triangle and continue until the first row has been finished. In making the second row, be careful to have the point of each lower triangle exactly against the center of the base of triangle on the next row.

Point "D"—This is a combination of the half stitch and buttonhole stitch. One row is made in the same manner as Point "A",

except that three instead of two stitches are made when cording, so that the size may be larger. The second row is then made with buttonhole stitch by means of stitches very close together which must be located between the row of half stitches and the filler. Fill in all the space in this way, alternating the two points. Continue towards the right, repeating the different points in the same order as they were first made.

Then begin the little bars, making them with a double stitch, cut out the organdie in the large circle sufficiently to make the bar. Take two lines of running stitches and make the bar with the aid of two strands when using a double stitch. Continue cutting out and making bars between the two larger circles until completed and maintain the distances as shown in the photograph.

Then cut out the material in the space between points "A" and "B" and take a line of running stitches from "E" to "F", returning with another line of stitches to the starting point, that is to say "E". In this way the spaces will be divided into two equal parts.

Start from this point to make four bars as shown in the photograph, taking two lines of stitches and with two strands of thread from the machine, finish with a double stitch and loop as indicated in Lesson 17—"Bone Lace—First Applique".

Baste a strand of darning cotton around the outline of the star and around both circles, and with a double strand of thread from the machine make a buttonhole stitch. Afterward cut out the material from the inside of the smaller circle, take two lines of running stitches at each of the diagonal lines, using double stitch. Finally make a broken line with two lines of running stitches and finish it with a double stitch and loops.

MATERIAL: Organdie.

THREADS: Embroidery No. 80 in the needle and in the bobbin.
For the outline—Darning Cotton.

NEEDLE: No. 8.

TENSIONS: The upper tension moderate and the bobbin tension a little tight.

Shaded Embroidery

THIS embroidery differs from all the others that have been explained heretofore, as it is not made in accordance with either Rule No. 1 or Rule No. 2. It is produced in an entirely different manner. The hoops are carried forward and backward but they should never be turned sideways and the stitches are invariably two forward and one backward. By this combination of stitches the point known as "Silk Point" is produced. This point is unique and does not permit of any variation.

It is adviasble to select a model or plate in colors which will serve as guide for the

different gradings of shades and also so as to enable the operator to keep an adequate assortment of colored silks. It must be made on satin, as in this case, or moire of good quality, and placing on the wrong side of the material a piece of nainsook or some other similar material to serve as reinforcement. It can also be made on cotton crepe, washable silk, net, etc., using as a reinforcement organdie or cambric. In the latter case, after the work has been finished, the reinforcing material must be cut out to avoid being seen through the work which would impair its beautiful appearance.

Prepare the machine with Embroidery Thread No. 60 in the bobbin and sewing silk No. 00 in the needle. Needle No. 9. The upper tension to be moderate and the bobbin tension a little tight.

Draw the pattern on the material acording to General Instructions and make a line of stitching over the entire outline, using the lightest shade of silk corresponding to each section, that is to say, green for the stem and the leaves and rose for the petals.

Begin with the part of the flower that appears to be farthest and that is only partly covered on the other side. In the design shown in the photograph the stem should be made first by shading it with stitches on the bias, then proceeding with the leaf on the right hand side which is partly covered by a petal. After this continue with the leaf on the left hand side and finally the one that is underneath.

Now continue with the petals, beginning in the center of the upper part of one of them with a light shade made in the direction of the calyx of the flower, taking stitches of about ⅕ of an inch, then go upwards toward the edge with two stitches and return with one stitch which should be short or long according to the variation in color and shading of the design. Baste with a second tone of somewhat darker shading and proceed to blend the long and short stitches with the first ones that were taken. Shading in this manner the first two colors in accordance with the pattern. Now proceed with the third shade, which should serve as a dividing line for the petals, and continue shading.

The folds of the petals are made by filling in the spaces with long stitches. Then draw a strand of silk from the needle to be used as a filler and do the raised embroidery with stitches on the bias, shading as the plate may call for. After all the material included in the hoops has been finished, and before removing it, moisten on the wrong side and iron it after having cut all the loose threads.

We suggest that the long and short stitches be properly combined following the vein of the leaf or the petals, by carrying the hoops in such a way that the stitches are always taken in the direction of the operator.

MATERIAL: Satin reinforced with Nainsook.
THREADS: In the bobbin, Embroidery No. 60.
In the needle, Sewing Silk No. 00.
NEEDLE: No. 9.
TENSIONS: The upper tension moderate, the bobbin tension a little tight.

SINGER

INSTRUCTIONS

FOR

ART EMBROIDERY

AND

LACE WORK

SECOND COURSE

OF

STUDY

▼▼

SINGER SEWING MACHINE COMPANY

Teneriffe Wheels

THIS lace is very popular on account of its elegance and delicate workmanship. Each one of the wheels must be made separately and then they can be joined and used in the making of insertions, lace, circles, etc. It is made on organdie or similar material. No importance is to be attached to the quality of the material since it will disappear entirely.

Thread Silk No. 00 can be used or Embroidery Thread No. 80 combined with Sewing Thread No. 200, changing according to the taste of the operator and the particular use for which the work is intended.

After placing the material in the hoops well stretched and having all its threads in a straight line, draw a circle of about 4 inches in diameter, which is divided into four equal parts, marking with carbon pencil small lines on the outside of the outline at the place marked in the photograph "A", "B", "C" and "D".

Prepare the machine with Embroidery Thread

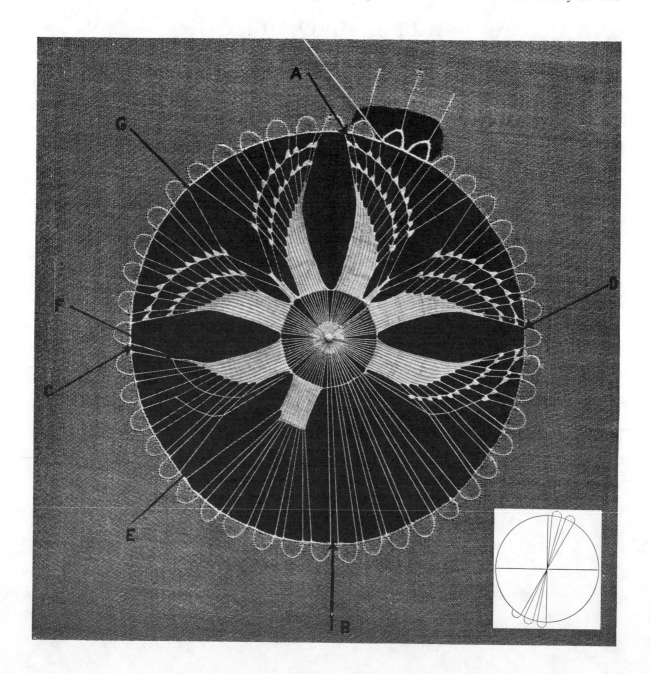

No. 80, both in the needle and in the bobbin. Use needle No. 8. The upper tension to be moderate and the bobbin tension somewhat tight. Take a line of stitches all over the outline and then carrying as a filler a single thread; reinforce the line of stitching made, then change the threads inserting No. 200 sewing thread both in the needle and in the bobbin, and using the same needle. Tensions to be even and moderate. Cut out the interior of the material around the line of the circle from about $1/5$ of an inch, to the left of "A", passing beyond "D" up to a distance of about $1/5$ of an inch beyond "B". In other words, leave sufficient space to cross the first line of running stitches from "A" to "B" and take the stitches in accordance with the Table of Stitches.

Fasten the line of running stitching with two or three stitches and when getting to "B" cut the threads and tie them on the wrong side of the material. Cut the material from "B to "A" passing the second line of running stitches between "C" and "D" and continue over the material, forming a little loop of about $1/5$ of an inch wide and of the same length. Continue until reaching the opposite side without cutting the threads and using the same care as when you were making hemstitching (Lessons Nos. 6 and 7), in passing over the central points. When getting to the other end repeat the loops and continue in this way until all the threads have been crossed as may be observed in the enlarged part of the section shown in the photograph. The distance between each loop must be $1/14$ of an inch and the number of threads must be even.

Change the threads again both in the needle and in the bobbin, using embroidery thread No. 80. The tension of the bobbin should be a little tighter. To begin the darning make the center as explained in Lessons 6 and 7. Take four turns near the center, moving the hoops with a circular motion and crossing two threads at each stitch, then take another four turns, darning the threads separately which will produce the result as shown in the photograph.

When the center has been finished, cut the threads and tie them. Take a line of stitches at a distance of $1/3$ of an inch from the center to form the circle and from this circle start the darning as per sample.

After all the darning has been made, continue with the ornamental part. Begin at "E" and take a line of stitching following the design up to "F", where it should be fastened with a stitch in the shape of a cross, From there continue with the triangle darnings, which should be made in succession; then cut the threads and tie, repeat this operation until all the ornamental triangles have been completed, then make all the darning as indicated by "G".

The next step will be to reinforce the loops. This will be done by carrying a single thread from the machine as a filler, after which cut the outside of the material at a distance of about $1/5$ of an inch from the edge. With a line of stitching reach the material and penetrate to a certain distance with several stitches which will serve as a support to preserve the proper shape of the loops. Now cut the material from the interior of the loops and cord them, using as a filler thread taken from the machine. The outline of the circle should be done in the same way and finally cut the stitches that were taken in the material which served as supports.

When making this lace directly on a piece of material where it will stay, there is no necessity to cut out the outside of the loops, but simply cord them. This can be done if the material is organdie, silk or some other material of similar nature, but if it is heavy material then the lace should be made on one of the thin materials and then applied to the work.

MATERIAL: Organdie.

THREADS: To cross the Thread No. 200 both in the needle and in the bobbin. For the outline Darning and Cording, Embroidery No. 80 in the needle and in the bobbin.

NEEDLE: No. 8.

TENSIONS: For crossing the threads, both moderate and even. For the darning and cording, the upper tension moderate and bobbin tension somewhat tight.

Mexican Drawn Work

THIS work is similar to hemstitching and not much more difficult but more complicated on account of the combination of threads. When finished it is particularly strong, which permits its application to articles of practical use in the home, such as towels, bed linen, table covers, etc.

To obtain the best results it is necessary to select material having threads running straight from one end to the other and more or less of the same thickness, as this has very much to do with the final satisfactory result.

Prepare the machine with Embroidery Thread No. 40 in the bobbin and No. 60 in

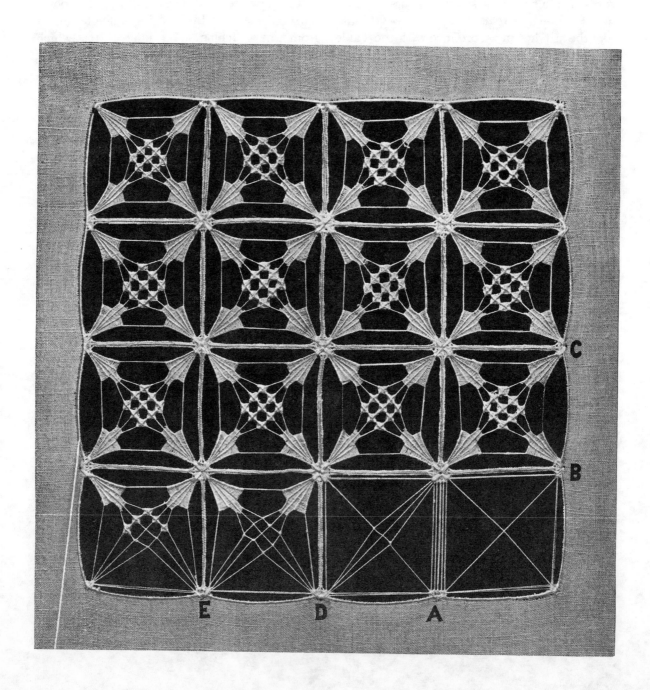

the needle. Needle No. 9. Both tensions moderate and even.

The material shown in the sample is linen. The size of each square of lace work should first be indicated and then draw one thread from each of its sides. Threads are drawn from a space of about one inch, leave 1/5 of an inch without drawing, and repeat the same operation over the whole square. After doing this in one direction, do likewise in the opposite direction, thus forming squares, after which the work can be placed in the hoops, seeing that the dividing threads are straight and even at the ends. Release two threads from the edge of the material in order that the darning may be uniform, and reinforce the four sides of the square. Then proceed to make five small groups of hemstitching on each side, that is to say, in the space of about one-fifth of an inch that was provided for the separation between each square and repeating this operation in other small squares at the center. Consult the photograph.

To make the first diagonal line of stitchings begin at "A", where the threads will be fastened, go to "B" and slightly reinforce the edge until you reach "C". From that point take a line of running stitches up to "D" and there fasten with 3 stitches, taking care in crossing the angles of the material that was left for the separation between squares, fasten the stitching with five stitches one in the center, the second backwards in the space of the angle, coming back to the place where the first stitch was taken. The fourth stitch is taken forward also in the space and return with a last stitch, so as to join the center where the other stitches were already taken. Continue in the same manner until all the squares are divided with diagonal stitching and repeat in an opposite direction, beginning at "E".

After the crossing of the diagonal lines has been concluded, take another line of stitching, beginning at "D" (see the square "D"—"A"). This line on arriving at the opposite diagonal must be secured with three stitches at a distance of 1/7 of an inch from the center. Take care that this same distance is maintained all the way through the work. Continue with this stitching until finished. Then begin with the third, proceeding in an identical manner as was done with the second, except that the fastening is made on the other side of the center.

The lines of running stitches going in an opposite direction are made in like manner. In this way four small squares are formed in the center of each square. These little squares will be perfect if the same distance has been preserved between the lines of running stitches (See square "E" to "D").

The balance of the work simply consists in making darning stitch as was explained in Hemstitching, Lessons No. 6 and No. 7, the only variation being in the small darning at the squares, which consists in fastening the stitching with one stitch taken over each thread that crosses. This is done so as to obtain the square shape. Finally cord the edges, carrying as a filler one strand of darning cotton.

Be careful to closely follow the sample shown in the photograph, so as to preserve the good appearance of the work.

MATERIAL: Linen.
THREADS: Embroidery No. 40 in the bobbin. Embroidery No. 60 in the needle. To cord the edges—Darning Cotton.
NEEDLE: No. 9.
TENSIONS: Moderate and even. For darning the bobbin tension should be a little tight.

Hedebo Embroidery

THIS embroidery is very substantial and in good taste. It consists of small bars of running stitches, lace and cording with loops, and is particularly adapted for table linens, cushions, pillows, etc. It may also be combined with other styles of embroidery. It can be made on any kind of material.

The sample shown in the photograph was made on linen batiste.

Machine should be prepared with Embroidery Thread No. 60 in the bobbin and No. 80 in the needle. Needle No. 8. The needle tension should be moderate and that of the bobbin a little tight.

After the material has been placed in the hoops, trace the design in accordance with General Instructions, and then take a line of stitching over the outline and

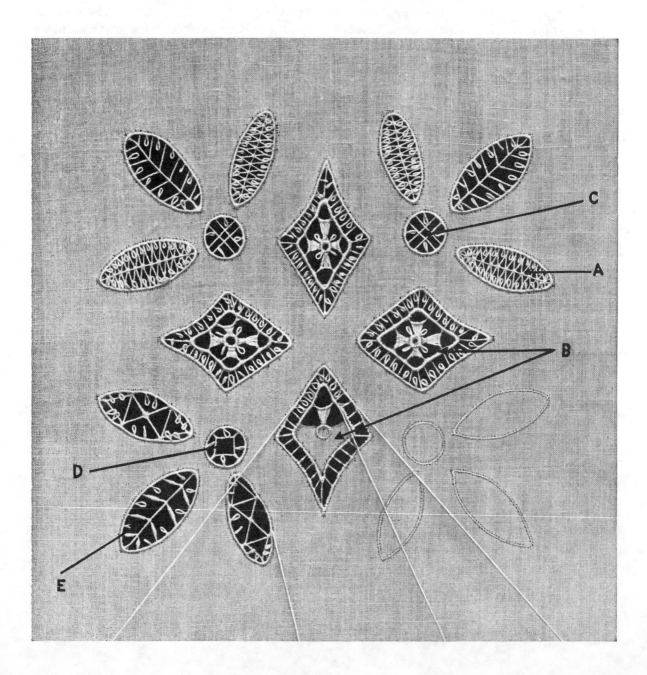

reinforce with a thread from the machine.

Point "A"—Cut out the material over the entire outline. At a distance of about $\frac{1}{12}$ of an inch from one of the ends, take a line of running stitches in zig-zag crossing the design from one end to the other and cord this line, taking a strand of double thread from the machine. This operation is repeated, taking a second line of running stitches in a zig-zag but in an opposite direction. Then take a third line which should be run over the center joining the crossing of both zig-zags. After this draw double strand of thread from the machine and return over the same line, cording it, making tiny circles of darning at each of the crossings above mentioned. With a strand of Irish Thread No. 70, cord the edge, making a little loop in the space between each one of the zig-zag threads. The explanation of this loop was given in Lesson 17 ("Bone Lace—First Applique").

Point "B"—Cut out the material little by little as you are cording the small bars and continue until this cording has been completed. Also cut out sufficient material from the inside to make the small bar which closes the angle. This bar is made by taking a line of stitches, uniting both interior edges, and then cording. Continue cutting out material until you reach the stitching that makes the circle in the center. From that point take lines of running stitches to the small bar. This line of stitching should be further apart at the connection with the bars then in the center. Take two stitches at the point close to the circle so as to join them. Proceed in the same manner with the other three angles. After this cut out the material from the circle and cord it with a strand of Irish Thread No. 70 and make four loops, one between each group of the running stitches taken. Finally cord the sides of the interior square the same as those of the exterior and make loops over the latter.

Point "C"—Cut out the material and take two parallel lines of stitching in one direction and cord them, repeating the operation in an opposite direction, then cord the outline of the circle in the same way as was done at Point "A", and insert one little loop in every other space.

Point "D"—This point is known as "Spirit Point". Cut out the material and divide the circumference into four equal parts. Start with a line of stitching from one of the points which have been marked and when reaching the nearest point, fasten the threads, turn the hoops and continue until reaching the next point, joining this line of stitching with the one that was made before. Reinforce both of them to a length of about $\frac{1}{25}$ of an inch forming a corner. Continue with this stitching and fasten it at the edge of the circle returning to the starting point where the stitches should be joined. Finish cording them with a filler of double thread from the machine, taking care that the little diamond in the center is properly formed. The loops are to be made in the usual way.

Point "E"—Cut out the material and from the upper angle take a line of running stitches, crossing the space from one end to the other and being careful that this line of running stitches is in the center of the space. From the point where the line terminated, draw a double strand of thread from the machine and cord the stitching to the point where the tapering bars of raised embroidery are to be placed. These tapering bars are made by taking a line of stitching from the edge to the point indicated and cording it without any filler. When getting to about half the length of the tapering bar, take several stitches on top of each other, so as to obtain the required thickness, then continue with ordinary stitching until reaching the central line of stitching and fasten the threads there. Repeat the same operation on the opposite side so as to form pairs of tapering bars in a diagonal direction, cording the center line until reaching the next two tapering bars. The entire section is to be made in the same way. The loops are to be made as explained before.

MATERIAL: Linen Batiste.
THREADS: In the bobbin, Embroidery No. 60.
        In the needle, Embroidery No. 80.
        For the edges—Irish Thread No. 70.
NEEDLE: No. 8.
TENSIONS: The needle tension moderate, the bobbin tension a little tight.

Velvet Applique

AMONG the great variety of artistic embroidery that can be accomplished on the sewing machine, that known as "Velvet Applique" is one of the prettiest and simplest. By studying the sample reproduced in the photograph, an idea will be gained of the good effect obtainable by enlarging this kind of work and applying it on curtains, cushions, table covers, etc.

The machine should be prepared with Embroidery Thread No. 60 in the bobbin and silk thread No. 00 in the needle of the

same color as the satin which is to be used. Needle No. 9. The upper tension moderate and the bobbin tension a little tight.

Place the velvet on the satin, both of them being well stretched in the hoops. Then trace the design on transparent paper which should be placed on the velvet, taking a line of stitching around the outline. Remove the paper carefully and take a second line of stitching close to the first and cut out the velvet around the outline, preserving it only in such spaces as are indicated in the design. Reinforce the edges where the material was cut out and cord the lines of the design, using three double strands of darning cotton of the same shade as the silk thread No. 00 and following instructions contained in Rule No. 2.

In order that the stem may be neatly finished, raised embroidery should be made with stitches on the bias. When the work has been completed, iron it on the wrong side but do not press very hard.

The sample reproduced was made by placing the velvet on the satin. This kind of work can also, if desired, be made by reversing the method, that is placing the satin on the velvet.

MATERIAL: Satin and Velvet.
THREADS: In the bobbin, Embroidery No. 60.
In the needle, Silk No. 00.
For the edges—Darning Cotton.
NEEDLE: No. 9.
TENSIONS: The upper tension moderate and the bobbin tension a little tight.

Battenberg Embroidery

AMONG the many fancy embroideries on white goods, the Battenberg variety is one of the most attractive. It is composed of a combination of points which lends considerable artistic merit to it. It is recommended for many uses, for example—on table linen, cushions, table covers, curtains, etc.

Any kind of closely woven goods may be used. The sample in the photograph was made on linen batiste.

The machine is to be prepared with No. 60 Embroidery Thread in the bobbin and No. 80 Embroidery Thread in the needle. Needle No. 8. Both tensions moderate and even for

the darning work. For the balance of the work the upper tension moderate and the bobbin tension a little tight.

Place the material in the hoops, well stretched, and trace the design in accordance with the General Instructions. Take a line of stitching and then reinforce with a thread from the machine over all the part of the outline which is going to be cut out. After the material has been cut out take lines of running stitches and darning the same way as was done in Lessons 6 and 7 "Hemstitching". Complete one section before beginning the next.

Each section should be finished with three small scallops. Continue the darning until the first scallop has been finished and take eight or ten stitches of about $1/12$ inch long inwards, continuing to the next scallop and repeating the operation, then finishing the edge. These long stitches should be taken in the same row where the darning is made so that the scallops, which should be well pronounced, will be uniform.

The section is completed by taking two lines of running stitches and making at each crossing of the threads a small darned square similar to the interior small squares of the Mexican Drawn Work—Lessons 27 and 28.

The center of the design is to be embroidered afterwards. You will notice it contains the points explained in Lesson 13—"English Lace", and Point "F" of Lessons 10 and 11, "Fancy Stitches on White Goods".

Finally, raised embroidery is to be made wherever required, according to the design, by placing the filling as per instructions contained in Lesson 9,"Letters and Monograms".

MATERIAL: Batiste Linen.

THREADS: In the bobbin, No. 60 Embroidery.
In the needle, No. 80 Embroidery.

NEEDLE: No. 8.

TENSIONS: For the raised cording, the needle tension should be moderate and the bobbin tension a little tight. For the darning—both tensions moderate and even.

Applique of Cretonne

THIS work consists in applying cut out cretonne flowers or figures on net, satin, or colored linen. The applique forms groups or garlands and is applied with shaded embroidery stitches. This work is particularly suitable for cushions, bed spreads, curtains, table covers, etc.

In order to make the raised effect more noticeable and to enhance its beauty, several stitches should be taken with colored silk of the same colors as those of the goods. If these stitches are taken in an artistic way, they will give the impression of having been painted.

The sample reproduced in the photograph shows a combination of flowers and leaves applied on net.

Prepare the machine with embroidery thread No. 60 in the bobbin, Needle No. 9, and silk thread No. 00 of the same color as the material. Tensions both moderate and even.

Place the net on the organdie which will serve as reinforcement, put upon it the cretonne design selected, take a line of stitching around the outline and cut out the extra material close to the edges. Then take another line of stitching to reinforce. With colored silk take several shaded stitches which should start from the edge of the applique towards the center, proceeding in the same manner as indicated in Lessons 24 and 25—"Shaded Embroidery", that is to say, two stitches forward and one backward.

These stitches must be made over all the outline of the leaves, the stem and petals, also in the folds or in the several shadings in the center, changing the colors of the silks for others of lighter or darker shades as the design may call for, the purpose being to have the edges stand out.

The veins of the leaves should be made with stitches on the bias and with silk of a darker color than that of the leaf in order that it may stand out quite clearly. After the embroidery has been finished cut out the organdie and the figure will remain appliqued on the net.

The organdie should be placed on the wrong side and is utilized only as a base or reinforcement when working on flimsy materials.

If the piece of work is large, place the material well stretched on a table and distribute the cuttings of cretonne, either flowers or figures, wherever they belong and then baste them into position. After this proceed as has already been explained.

By carefully studying the photograph you will obtain a clear conception of this fancy work.

MATERIALS: Net, organdie and cretonne.

THREADS: In the bobbin, Embroidery No. 60. In the needle, Silk No. 00.

NEEDLE: No. 9.

TENSIONS: Both moderate and even.

Blond Lace

THIS is one of the few laces in which black net with a small and round mesh is used and it is generally suitable for veils, mantillas, etc.

The machine is to be prepared with Needle No. 9, Black Silk Thread No. 00 in the needle and the same thread number in the bobbin. Tensions are to be moderate and even.

After placing the net in the hoops, trace the design as explained in General Instructions and begin by taking a line of stitching and a second line to reinforce the first over the entire outline, carrying a filler of one thread from the machine in reinforcing the outline where lace "A" is made.

Do the stitching to fill in the design in the

direction that may be required. The stitches are to be taken somewhat close together at some places and at other places slightly apart from each other, so as to produce the effect of a transparent fabric.

At the space indicated by "A" make the "Half Stitch Bone Lace Point". Cut out the net little by little as you proceed with the work, make lines of running stitches parallel to each other from edge to edge of the design. These lines of stitching must be at an equal distance from each other of about $1/25$ of an inch. After this run lines of stitching in an opposite direction, taking a stitch between each thread. After the little squares have been finished make lines of running stitches in a diagonal direction. These stitches should not be started from the corners of the little squares but a little distance from the sides of the squares, always maintaining uniformity.

When cording the outlines make the small loops shown in the photograph. These loops are to be placed at a distance of about $1/12$ of an inch to $1/9$ of an inch from each other.

MATERIAL: Black net of small and round mesh.
THREADS: Black silk No. 00 both in the needle and in the bobbin.
NEEDLE: No. 9.
TENSIONS: Both moderate and even.

Valenciennes Lace

MANY beautiful combinations can be made with this style of lace. It is, therefore, very suitable for the ornamentation of underwear and is used on many different garments.

It is made on net of small and round mesh.

The machine is prepared with embroidery thread No. 80 in the bobbin and embroidery thread No. 100 in the needle. Needle No. 7. Both tensions are to be moderate and even, except for the cording when the tension of the bobbin must be somewhat tight.

After the design has been traced, take a line of stitching over the outline and another line of reinforced stitching.

Carry as a filler a single thread from the machine, reinforcing those parts where the lace points are made. Also an interior line of stitching is to be made so as to indicate parts where the lace is to be executed, as in this lace there must be left a free space inwards of about $1/25$ of an inch on both edges. (See the photograph).

Begin the lace by covering with stitching the spaces that are to serve as outlines, taking care to have the stitches very close together. Then make the small lace points as per photograph and cut out the net little by little as you proceed with the work, bearing in mind in the making of the Bone Lace Stitch or Half Stitch the instructions contained in Lesson 33 "Blond Lace". Finally cord the edges with a filler of Irish Thread No. 80 and using the same filling make little loops at a distance of about $1/25$ of an inch from each other.

MATERIAL: Net of small and round mesh.
THREADS: In the bobbin, Embroidery No. 80. In the needle, Embroidery No. 100. For the cording and the little loops, Irish Thread No. 80.
NEEDLE: No. 7.
TENSIONS: Both moderate and even, except for the cording where the bobbin tension must be a little tight.

Cluny Lace

THIS style of lace is of considerable beauty and adaptable for a great variety of work. It is especially suitable in the preparation of delicate pieces of work on net of small and round mesh. Because of its characteristic features it requires a design consisting of compact figures and with small spaces in the background.

The machine should be prepared with Embroidery Thread No. 80 in the bobbin and in the needle. Needle No. 8. For the stitching and the points on the net, both tensions should be moderate and even, and for the cording the upper tension should be moderate and the bobbin tension a little tight.

The design is to be traced according to

instructions in Lesson 18 "Embroidery on Net", using the same precautions so as to obtain the necessary tightness of the net and also to prevent the design from losing its shape. Take a line of stitching over all the outline, carefully remove the paper and carry as a filler a single thread from the machine to reinforce the stitching. Then begin to embroider the points and the lace work as shown in the photograph.

Point "A"—Take a line of stitching to divide this section lengthwise into two equal parts. Draw a strand of thread from the machine to serve as a filler and with stitches on top of each other make the zig-zag as shown in the photograph.

Point "B"—Take three or more stitches at an equal distance from each other until one section has been entirely covered.

Point "C"—Consists only in filling in a space with stitches very close together. Continue in this way, alternating the points in subsequent sections until all the sections which form the flowers have been finished. Then proceed with the lace work at Point "D" in the center. Cut out the net and in the space left make two interwoven zig-zag lines which should be corded over a thread drawn from the machine. Then make the lines of stitching to cross the zig-zag and the little bar that divides this section into two parts. Draw a strand of thread from the machine and cord the stitching up to a distance of $1/_{25}$ of an inch from the crossing with the zig-zag and, at that point, stopping the needle for a moment, take a line of stitching forming a circle which will be finished at its starting point. At the latter point again take a strand of thread as a filler and continue to the edge. Repeat the same procedure at the other crossing and finish by cording the little bar.

After the above has been done, cord the outlines with a strand of crochet thread No. 30 and leave the material in the hoops, and cut out the net in the spaces indicated, as may be seen in the photograph, as closely as possible to the edge but taking care not to damage the work.

MATERIAL: Net with small and round mesh.

THREADS: Embroidery No. 80 both in the needle and in the bobbin.
For the cording, Crochet Thread No. 30.

NEEDLE: No. 8.

TENSIONS: For the stitching and points on the net, both moderate and even. For the cording, upper tension moderate and the bobbin tension a little tight.

Fancy Lace

EDUCATION and culture bring about a refinement of taste, and, therefore, the demand for embroidery work is becoming greater daily and the possibilities under the head of remuneration could not be better. The ease with which this work can be done on the Singer Machine makes possible the transformation of simple material into beautiful pieces of work, and this has contributed to transform embroidery from the simple art of the home that it was heretofore into an industry and a source of income for many families.

The sample of embroidery reproduced in the photograph confirms the above. It is particularly adapted for cushions, bed spreads, underwear, curtains, etc. It is made on cotton crepe, washable silk or organdie, and

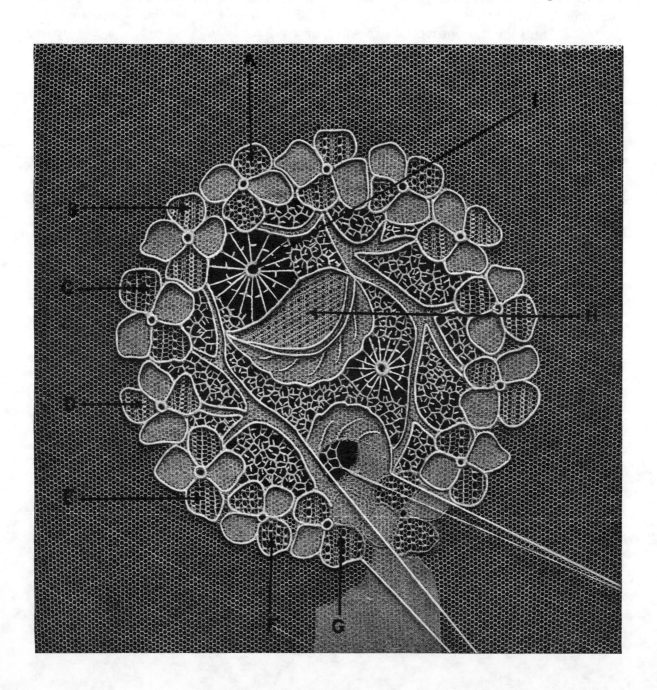

as a base net with small and round mesh should be used.

The sample reproduced was made on organdie. Place the organdie on the net and insert both into the hoops, taking care that both materials are well stretched. Trace the design following General Instructions.

The machine should be prepared with Needle No. 8, embroidery thread No. 80 in the needle and the same thread and number in the bobbin. Both tensions are to be moderate and even for the points. For the lace work in the background and for the cording the upper tension should be moderate and the bobbin tension somewhat tight.

Begin by taking a line of stitching over the outline and then reinforce with a single thread filler from the machine. Afterward cut out the organdie of two petals of each flower as may be seen in the photograph and then the net will be ready to be worked.

Point "A"—This point is similar to Point "H" of Lesson 18, "Embroidery on Net", except that one row of meshes is left unworked for each one that is embroidered.

Point "B"—Cord the meshes of one row, skip one, and at the next take two lines of running stitches parallel to each other, continue alternating in this manner until the petal has been finished.

Point "C"—This is made by taking two threads of each mesh in one row and cording them with several stitches, taken on top of each other. Continue in this way until the entire row has been finished. Skip two rows and then reinforce the threads of the meshes where these come in contact with the next row.

Point "D"—Embroider the meshes just the same as those at Point "C" with the exception that one thread only should be taken. Skip one row and at the next row take two lines of running stitches parallel to each other.

Point "E"—This is a combination of Points "C" and "D".

Point "F"—The method to do this point is identical with that explained in connection with Point "C" with the only exception that no space should be left between the rows of meshes.

Point "G"—This is made by combining a row of meshes, as per Point "C", with one row of running stitches as explained under Point "D". Then cut out the center of the flower and cord.

Point "H"—After the flowers have been completed, proceed to make the leaf, cut out the organdie in the middle of the leaf and make Point "H" as per Lesson No. 18, with the difference that in this case it should be made in a diagonal direction instead of horizontal. At the other half of the leaf the veins are to be made with stitches on the bias.

To make the irregular lace points in the background cut out the net and the organdie little by little as you proceed with the work so that the design may not lose its proper shape, then draw a strand from the machine to be used as a filler but do not cut the larger spaces as in point "I" until the entire background has been formed. Now you can make the small bars with picot edge effect and which start from Point "I". This should not be done however until a reinforced line of stitching with one strand of thread has been made.

After all the little bars have been completed around the circle, cut out the interior and cord with a strand of thread from the machine.

To make the little picot work proceed as follows: Cord the small bar half way and take a thread to be placed alongside at a distance of $1/25$ of an inch, take a stitch connecting the strand of thread and return over the same strand, cording it with two or three stitches until reaching the starting point. Then draw the strand of thread and the small picot will remain loose. Continue by cording the little bar. Cut out the center of each flower and cord it. Finally neatly cord all the outline, using as a filler Irish Thread No. 80.

MATERIAL: Organdie, Net with a small and round mesh.

THREADS: Embroidery No. 80 both in the needle and in the bobbin.
For the outlines—Irish Thread No. 80.

NEEDLE: No. 8.

TENSIONS: For the points, both moderate and even.
For the lace work in the background and for the cording, the needle tension should be moderate and the bobbin tension a little tight.

English Point Lace

THE reproduction in the photograph will convey an idea of the delicate work involved in this class of embroidery which has enumerable uses. It is made on net of a small and round mesh. Organdie should be used over the net as a reinforcement to prevent the work from stretching and losing its shape.

Prepare the machine with embroidery thread No. 80 in the bobbin and in the needle. Use needle No. 8. For the first part of the work, that is to say, the points on the net, the tensions are to be moderate and even, and for the background and the cording, the bobbin tension should be somewhat tight.

After placing the net and the organdie in the hoops, trace the design in accordance with General Instructions and take a line of stitch-

ing around the outline and reinforce it with a single thread filler taken from the machine.

In making the points on the net cut out the organdie little by little as you proceed with the work so as to preserve the exact shape of the design. There are many different points that can be used with good effect in this work, but we recommend using the points indicated in the photograph, at least in the beginning.

Point "A"—Reinforce the meshes of the net in a spiral shape taking alternate meshes from opposite sides. In this way, at the next row, make a cording, taking one thread from the mesh, and at the third row repeat the spiral shape. Proceed in this manner until all sections which call for this point have been completed.

Point "B"—Take two lines of stitching parallel to each other in the same row, skip one and at the next take two more lines of parallel stitching, and continue in the same way until the entire background of this section has been finished. Stitching in a diagonal direction, take one stitch at each crossing with the lines of stitching in the background and make tiny knots, skip one row and repeat, alternating until the whole space has been completed. Then beginning in an opposite direction, make a diagonal line of stitching, taking the first stitch at the same place where the previous one was fastened.

Point "C"—Make two lines of stitching as explained in Point "B" to form the background, then make a diagonal line of stitching which should connect with two stitches the threads of two meshes when the rows of unworked meshes are crossed. When reaching the parallel lines of stitching in the background, make little knots by taking nine stitches at each one of these points.

Point "D"—Reinforce the meshes in a spiral line and repeat in an opposite direction. At each point of crossing with the previous line take five stitches so as to produce a chain effect of small links.

Point "E"—This is the only point in this lesson that is made in the direction contrary to that of the meshes. Cord the thread which joins the meshes, when reaching the next mesh take two stitches so as to close it entirely, then take a stitch backwards in a diagonal

direction. Return forward with another stitch and again backward with a diagonal stitch, finishing with a stitch forward. Continue by reinforcing the thread up to the next mesh where you will repeat what has been explained until completing the row, and the same thing should be done with each one of the rows in this section. Be careful that the spots at each subsequent row alternate with those of the previous row; in other words, no two consecutive rows should have the spots in similar places.

Point "F"—Take a line of stitching in a zig-zag over a row of meshes. In making this line of stitching, two stitches must be taken which will cover about one-half the mesh on the right hand side and two stitches covering half of the next mesh on the left hand side, then two stitches on the right half of the next mesh, and so on until the entire row has been completed. Skip one row and in the next repeat the zig-zag. Continue until the whole background of the section has been executed. Then make in the first row, that was left undone, tiny hemstitching in zig-zag, which is made by taking three stitches to cover half the mesh on one side, and at the next mesh covering half the mesh on the opposite side. Skip one row and at the next repeat the zig-zag hemstitching.

After all the points have been finished, make the irregular background, which is one of the characteristic features of this kind of lace and which has already been explained in Lesson 36, ("Fancy Lace").

To conclude, cut out the organdie which may still be visible and cord the outside of the outline with a strand of Irish Thread No. 80.

MATERIALS: Net of small and round mesh.
　　　　　　Organdie as a reinforcement.
THREADS: Embroidery Thread No. 80 both in the needle and in the bobbin. To cord the outlines Irish Thread No. 80.
NEEDLE: No. 8.
TENSIONS: For the points on net, both moderate and even.
　　　　　　For the background and the cording, the upper tension moderate and the bobbin tension a little tight.

Artistic Embroidery on White Goods

THIS can be made on all kinds of material, from the finest to the heaviest, provided that the weave permits drawing of threads. The sample in the photograph was made on linen organdie of very fine quality.

After the material has been placed in the hoops, trace the design.

Prepare the machine with embroidery thread No. 80, both in the needle and in the bobbin. Needle No. 8. The upper tension to be moderate and the bobbin tension somewhat tight.

Take a line of short stitches around the outline of the design, draw a single thread from the machine, reinforce it and proceed with the fancy points.

Point "A"—Draw in a vertical direction eight threads and leave six, in the space thus formed make zig-zag hemstitching, following instructions contained in Lessons Nos. 6 and 7, ("Hemstitching").

Point "B"—Draw three threads in both directions and leave three.

Make two lines of running stitches in opposite diagonal directions which should

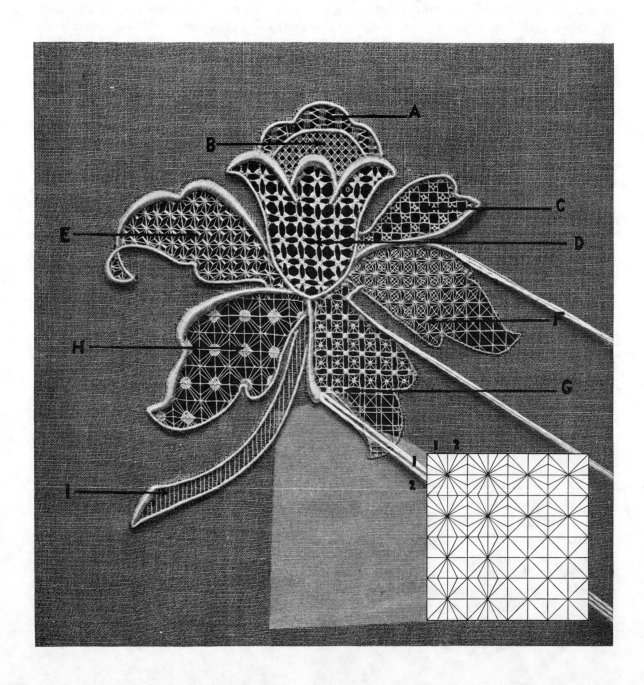

start, not from the corners of the squares, but from the sides at a little distance toward the center.

Point "C"—Draw four threads in both directions, leaving four which should be neatly corded so as to form meshes. To make the center of the small squares begin at the center of one of the sides and make a line of running stitches in a direction diagonal to one of the angles, repeat at the other three angles and reinforce with two stitches taken at the points where the diagonal lines join. In this way little diamonds will be produced in the interior which was made following diagonal lines in order not to cut the threads.

Point "D"—Draw eight threads in both directions and leave eight, take a stitch in the shape of a cross at the center where the threads cross each other so as to fasten them, and taking eight threads on each side make a darning stitch.

Point "E"—Draw in both directions eight threads and leave three which should be corded so as to form a mesh, make a diagonal line of stitching which should start from the angle of one of the small squares and cross all the others at their angles. Repeat this and make, at the same place, a second parallel line of stitching which should be fastened with one stitch at each crossing of the cording of the small squares in the mesh. The diagonal lines are made in one direction only. Take one of the vertical lines which form the mesh and reinforce up to the first angle; take one stitch at the right, connecting with the nearest diagonal thread which should be fastened at the angle; then repeat the operation towards the left, connecting with the nearest diagonal thread, which should also be fastened at the same angle. Continue reinforcing the vertical line until the next crossing or angle, where the operation should be repeated and so on until all the vertical lines have been completed.

Point "F"—Draw eight threads in both directions and leave three, which should be corded to form a mesh. Cross the opposite diagonal lines and finish in accordance with the instructions relative to "Mexican Drawn Work" (Lessons 27 and 28), forming in this way the small squares in the interior which will be seen in the photograph.

Point "G"—The method of drawing the threads for this point is somewhat different from that followed in making the other

points. Draw eight threads, leave two; draw two and leave two. Do the same thing in an opposite direction. Cord the threads so as to form the smaller and the larger squares and take two diagonal lines of stitching, one in each direction. At the center of each one of the large squares run two more lines of stitching at right angles, and over the crossing of these and of the diagonal lines already made, make a small circular darning as indicated in "First Openwork Stitches", (Lesson 4, Figure "D"). Finish by making a small raised square embroidered at each square.

Point "H"—Draw in both directions ten threads and leave three which should be corded to form a mesh, make diagonal lines in both directions at each intermediate angle in such a way that two angles of each square will remain uncrossed, then starting from points 1 and 2 (see the enlarged reproduction at the corner of the photograph), make two lines of zig-zag stitching, taking one stitch at each crossing over the lines already made so as to properly secure them. After making all the lines going in one direction, make those that go in an opposite direction. Be careful that the zig-zag stitching be as far as possible of the same size in all the lines so as to obtain uniform appearance. The circular and square darnings must be made alternately. Bear in mind, in connection with the square darnings, that the line of stitching must be secured with one stitch at each crossing of the corded threads of the mesh.

Point "I"—Draw two threads in a vertical direction and leave two, which should be corded, being careful to have the rows parallel.

To finish this work follow instructions given in the last part of Lesson 18 ("Embroidery on Net").

It is necessary to remember that in working on finer materials or on more closely woven fabric than that which was used in the sample reproduced, more threads will have to be drawn in proportion; on the contrary, if the material is heavier or with more open weave, fewer threads in proportion will have to be drawn.

MATERIAL: Organdie.

THREADS: Embroidery No. 80 both in the needle and in the bobbin.

NEEDLE: No. 8.

TENSIONS: The upper tension moderate and the bobbin tension a little tight.

Renaissance Lace

THIS is one of the most popular varieties for underwear, bed linen, shades, table covers and many other articles.

Sample reproduced was made on organdie. After being inserted into hoops the design is traced.

Prepare the machine with embroidery thread No. 80 in the needle and embroidery thread No. 60 in the bobbin. Needle No. 8. The upper tension should be moderate and the bobbin tension a little tight.

The braid is to be basted in accordance with instructions in Lesson 13 ("English

Lace") and now you will be ready to begin with the different points.

Point "A"—After the braid is placed in position cut out the interior of the material little by little and as you proceed with the meshes, which should be made by taking lines of running stitching in both directions from one edge to the other of the braid, be careful so that the design does not lose its shape. After the first section has been completed, continue with the next and so on until the entire space has been finished. Cord the threads of the mesh and then make the ornamental part, taking from three to five stitches in the shape of squares and according to the size desired.

Point "B"—Take lines of stitching in both directions at a distance of about $1/5$ of an inch from each other thus forming the mesh; then make two diagonal lines in an opposite direction as was explained in Lessons 39 and 40 ("Artistic Embroidery on White Goods"), Point "H", and then make the tapering bars which were described in Lesson 29 ("Hedebo Embroidery"), Point "E".

Point "C"—Cross the threads as was done in Point "B" and fasten them at the center where a small circular darning should be made. Take a line of stitching in the form of a circle at a distance of $1/12$ of an inch and then make the triangular darning shown in the photograph.

Point "D"—Take three lines of stitching at a distance of $1/25$ of an inch from each other and leave a space of $1/8$ of an inch, than take another three lines in the same direction and continue in this way until the entire space has been covered, both vertically and horizontally. Then make diagonal lines in the squares in both directions, taking at each crossing of the threads one stitch backwards which will have the effect of a knot.

Point "E"—Cross the threads in the same manner as at Points "B" and "C" and then make the small darning stitch shown in the photograph.

Point "F"—After all the meshes have been completed, the balance of the work is made, following instructions in connection with Point "E" of Lessons 39 and 40 ("Artistic Embroidery on White Goods").

The other sections are produced in accordance with instructions in Lesson 13.

MATERIAL: Organdie.
THREADS: In the bobbin, Embroidery Thread No. 60.
In the needle, Embroidery Thread No. 80.
NEEDLE: No. 8.
TENSIONS: The upper tension moderate and the bobbin tension somewhat tight.

Fancy Embroidery Points
on White Goods

THIS work is appropriate for glove cases, pictures, dresser sets and many other artistic purposes. It is a combination of many short points which have already been learned, such as hemstitching, raised embroidery, fancy lace points, etc., divided into sections and then properly applied.

The flower reproduced was made on lawn of a very close weave, but it can also be produced on practically any other material provided that it is closely woven.

The machine is to be prepared with embroidery thread No. 80 in the needle and in the bobbin. Needle No. 8. The upper tension should be moderate and the bobbin tension a little tight.

After the design has been traced on the material make a line of stitching all around the outline and reinforce with a filler of single thread from the machine. Then follow the procedure explained in connection with Point "F" of Lessons 10 and 11, ("Fancy

Stitches on White Goods"), draw eight threads in both directions from the center of the flower and leave four threads, forming small and even squares. Starting from the upper part take two of the vertical threads that were left and cord them, carrying as a filler a double thread which is drawn from the machine. This cording must be made up to the crossing with the threads that were left horizontal and at that crossing two stitches are to be taken in order to fasten the threads to the square. Cord two vertical threads of the side opposite that which was begun and continue cording until reaching the next crossing where the same operation of fastening should be repeated, and then continue with the side which was worked in the first place. Proceed in the same manner until the entire lot of vertical threads have been worked and then repeat on the two threads that were left uncorded. This operation must be made with all the threads that run in one direction and then with the others that cross the former, after which the outside outline should be corded. Finish by making the stem of the flower with raised embroidery stitch. This stem was made on the material as may be seen in the photograph and consists of two branches joined at the end.

Take another set of hoops where the appropriate material has been inserted. In this case the same material, that is, lawn of a very close weave, was used. Draw the design for Section "A", then take a line of stitching and another one to reinforce the outline, as was explained. Draw twelve threads and leave three in both directions and make the lace point explained in Lessons 39 and 40, ("Artistic Embroidery on White Goods"), Point "F". Cut out the material where the little bars are to be made in a zig-zag line, bearing in mind the instructions contained in Lesson 13 ("English Lace—Braid Applique"), and finish this section by cording all the outlines with a strand of Irish Thread No. 60 which should be carried tightly so as to give a certain body to the work.

In the same material, which can be utilized because the sections are small, trace the designs for Sections "B" and "C" and take a line of stitching and another to reinforce it, the same as was done with Section "A". Then begin the lace work at Section "B", drawing four threads and leaving four in both directions.

Afterward proceed with Section "C". This is made with fancy stitches similar to those indicated in Lessons 10 and 11, Point "B", but bear in mind that they must be made of the smallest possible size so as to obtain the required effect.

In conclusion, remove the material from the hoops, cut out, neatly, the edges, then apply in the first place Section "A" on the material and baste by means of a cording stitch. This stitching shall be covered when Sections "B" and "C" are applied. The latter sections will have to be corded in such a way as to convey the impression of standing separate. Notice "D" in the photograph which shows the cording which finally joins the three sections.

MATERIAL: Lawn of a very close weave.

THREADS: Embroidery No. 80, both in the needle and in the bobbin.
Irish Thread No. 60, for the cording.

NEEDLE: No. 8.

TENSIONS: The upper tension moderate, the bobbin tension a little tight.

Bone Lace—Insertions

THIS class of lace should satisfy the most fastidious, as, in addition to forming a harmonious combination of very good taste, it is delicate and flexible. The photograph clearly shows the process that should be followed in the production of the work from the first to the last stitch.

Use organdie as a base and trace the design in accordance with instructions previously given. Prepare the machine with embroidery thread No. 80 in the bobbin and in the needle and needle No. 8. Adjust the tensions to be moderate and even for the half stitch, for the darning and the leaves of bone lace; for the

small bars made with double stitch and for the buttonhole stitch, the bobbin tension should be a little tight.

Take a line of stitching over the outline of the design and reinforce it with a filler of single thread from the machine. Begin at Point "A", making parallel lines of running stitches and taking care that all of these lines are at a distance of about $\frac{1}{50}$ of an inch from each other, as shown in the photograph on the opposite page. Then make the lines in an opposite direction, crossing the first lines and taking one stitch between each thread when crossing the lines. In this way tiny squares with darning stitch will be formed.

Point "B" consists of the half stitch of bone lace and is made in the same manner as instructed in Lesson 33 ("Blond Lace").

Now proceed with the point at the edge. This point is made with lines of running stitches from one edge to the other, following the design and making them all at an equal distance from each other. Then make lines of stitching crossing the former and giving them the shape which the insertion calls for.

After the lace points have been completed, make the leaves, Point "C", following directions contained in Lesson 17, ("Bone Lace—First Applique").

To make the small bars and to finish the outline proceed in accordance with description in Lessons 19 and 20, ("Needle Point Lace and Venetian Richelieu Lace").

The insertion will now be ready to be applied on the work. This is done by fastening it to the material with buttonhole stitch, which is to be made on the outside of the insertion.

MATERIAL: Organdie.
THREADS: Embroidery No. 80, both in the needle and in the bobbin.
NEEDLE: No. 8.
TENSIONS: For the lace work and the leaves, both moderate and even; for the small bars and the buttonhole stitch, the upper tension moderate and the bobbin tension somewhat tight.

Fancy Lace Edging

THIS is a very appropriate lace for appli-cation on bed linen, underwear and many other similar garments.

Prepare the machine with sewing thread No. 200 in the bobbin and in the needle and needle No. 8. Both tensions are to be moder-ate and even.

As a base use organdie, on which you will trace the design exactly as per instructions given in Lesson 15 ("Filet Lace").

Make the lines of stitching which form the meshes and then change the tension of the bobbin, tightening it a little but leaving the upper tension moderate. Also change the

threads, inserting Embroidery Thread No. 80 both in the needle and in the bobbin.

Reinforce the meshes. For this purpose draw a single strand of thread from the machine and cord half of the meshes in a zig-zag line (see Guide of Point "A"); cord the opposite sides, making at the same time the little squares. To do this, when getting to Point "B" release the filler temporarily. Take a line of stitching so as to form the first square, again take the filler and with it cord the sides until getting to half of the third square and there again release the filler, take a straight line of stitching up to opposite edge and return, cording. Continue cording the side of the small square until you arrive at the point from which the next little bar starts and make this bar in the same way. Then cord the balance of the little square until returning to the starting point and repeat until finishing. Remember that the edges of the spaces where the tapering bars go are not reinforced; these are made as explained in connection with Point "E" of Lesson 29 ("Hedebo Embroidery").

Make the buttonhole stitching in the interior (see Point "C") using as a filler a double strand of thread from the machine and repeat over the exterior line and at the same time make the little loops which will be seen in the photograph. Finally cut out very neatly the ends of the mesh threads at the edges and in those parts which have not been worked.

MATERIAL: Organdie.

THREADS: For the meshes, Sewing Thread No. 200 both in the needle and in the bobbin. For the cording and the balance of the work, Embroidery Thread No. 80, both in the needle and in the bobbin.

NEEDLE: No. 8.

TENSIONS: For the meshes, both moderate and even. For the cording and the balance of the work, the upper tension moderate and the bobbin tension a little tight.

Bead Work

THIS style of work is most appropriate for border and flower designs. Both designs are largely used in dresses and ladies' hand bags, also on cushions, upholstery, etc. It is at times advisable to combine these designs with different fancy colors. The tracing of the design is to be made as per General Instruc-tions and according to the material to be used. The material may be silk, wool or satin.

The sample shown in the photograph was made on georgette crepe.

Prepare the machine with Embroidery Thread No. 60 in the bobbin, needle No. 9 and silk thread No. 00 of the same color as

the beads that are going to be applied.

The tensions to be moderate and even.

Insert the beads with the aid of a very fine sewing needle. Each color is to be inserted separately and the threads of silk must be long enough to permit the beads to run easily.

Begin by applying violet beads to form the first line of the border, taking a stitch between each bead. Then use the white beads and make a zig-zag line which will rest on the first line of violet beads. Now proceed to insert violet beads to form the inner part of the border.

Make the white triangles in the interior and apply violet beads to cover one side of the triangle as far as the vertics. At that point release temporarily the guide, leaving it properly secured ("A"), and with another string fill in the opposite side ("B"). When reaching the vertics with this second string fasten and cut it, then continue with the first string only.

To conclude apply the two strings of purple beads ("C") which form the edge of the border.

Now make the figures in the center. Apply the violet beads, working from the edge toward the center and leaving in the center a small space in the form of a diamond which should be filled in with white beads.

The designs requiring sky-blue beads are made in the same manner; that is to say, leaving at the center sufficient room for a line of white beads.

When reaching the places where the colors are to be changed care must be taken to fasten the threads with three or more stitches.

MATERIAL: Georgette Crepe.
THREADS: In the bobbin, Embroidery No. 60.
　　　　　In the needle, Silk No. 00.
NEEDLE: No. 9.
TENSIONS: Both somewhat tight and even.

Rococo Embroidery

ROCOCO Embroidery is a delicate and artistic piece of work. It is made with small ribbons known as "Rococo". These ribbons can be obtained in many colors and it is therefore possible to imitate flowers, leaves or any other designs that may be desired.

This type of embroidery is very appropriate for pieces of work of the Louis XV or Louis XVI styles, and can be made on materials ranging from the finest, such as net, to the heaviest, such as upholstery satin.

Copy the design on transparent paper, marking the stems with a line, the leaves with

a short line and wherever there is a flower just mark the center with a small circle and the length of the petals with lines.

Where the bow is to be placed mark it, showing its full surface and folds.

Wind the bobbin with Embroidery Thread No. 60. Use needle No. 9 which should be threaded with Green Silk No. 00, of the same color as the leaves. Tensions to be moderate and even.

Begin by making the leaves. See leaf half made on the right hand side at the bottom of the illustration. Fasten the threads on the line of the stem. Place the green ribbon in a horizontal position, crossing the line which indicates the leaf; make a line of stitching across the ribbon at the place marked by the line and return with a second line of stitching. Fold the ribbon backward over the part of ribbon already fastened, covering the stitching previously made. When getting to the stem, fasten under the ribbon with several stitches so as to give it the proper shape. Cut out the extra ribbon close to the stem. All other leaves are to be made exactly in the same manner.

Now make the stems with stitches on the bias, carrying as a filler a double silk thread from the machine.

Change the silk for another shade appropriate to that of the flower "A". Fasten the ribbon with a few stitches at one of the ends in the circle already indicated, take a line of stitching through the center of the ribbon covering the length of one petal, and from there another line of stitching crosswise. Return to the center with a line of stitching and fold ribbon over the previous folding upward about $1/12$ of an inch, which should be fastened with several stitches. This procedure is to be repeated until the entire flower is covered. The flower is finished with a small spot made with yellow silk. The petals should be side by side and the edges are all to be folded under in the same direction.

To make the Bud ("B") fasten the ribbon at the border of the central circle and begin by forming a small triangle. Turn the hoops and place several turns of ribbon around the triangle, fastening it conveniently. In placing the borders be careful to alternate the lighter

with the darker shades so as to produce correct tone of coloring. When finished cut and fold the ribbon in such a way that the end will be invisible.

Flower "C" is made by fastening the end of the ribbon and inserting it with one stitch into the border of the circle. Then turn it with a circular motion and hold it with the points of the scissors, continue until getting to the center close to the starting point and take another stitch the same as the first, forming in this way the first petal. After making the five petals shown in the photograph, make three small knots with yellow silk. These are made by taking one stitch in the center of the flower, leaving a loose strand of silk and making three turns very close together around the needle, then taking another stitch to tie them in order to form the little knot.

Letter "D"—Fasten the end of the ribbon in the center of the flower and take a line of stitching of the same length of the petal. Cover the line of stitching with ribbon and at that point fold under the ribbon and fasten it. Return with a line of stitching to the center. Turn the ribbon backwards covering the first ribbon and take another stitch so as to secure the edge at the circle. Continue with the other petals in the same way and finish the center with a small spot made of yellow silk.

Letter "E"—Make the petals in the same way as the leaves, increasing or decreasing the sizes in accordance with the design. Then at the center make a few knots in the same way as those made in flower "C", and conclude by making the two petals which cross the center and which cover the end of the first petals and part of the knots.

The bow is made the same as the flowers. Place the ribbon at the center, stitch over the lines indicated in the design and turn the ribbon so as to cover all those markings, continue until completed. Finally make a small knot so as to cover the ends of the ribbon.

MATERIAL: Satin.

RIBBON: Rococo.

THREADS: Embroidery No. 60 in the bobbin, Silk No. 60 in the needle.

NEEDLE: No. 9.

TENSIONS: Both moderate and even.

Venetian Embroidery

VENETIAN Embroidery is a variety of work of great originality on account of its form and artistic workmanship. It is different from any of those previously described, and it is suitable for sofa cushions, table and piano covers, etc.

It is advisable in the first place to consider the purpose for which the embroidery is to be made so as to select designs that may be appropriate inasmuch as the design itself is always repeated throughout the entire embroidery.

The design usually consists of stars or flowers with petals of straight lines, with slight

undulations or points connected by stems or lines which should be joined without leaving any loose ends. It may also consist of large flowers with petals of different shadings.

As a rule the sections dividing the petals are made in pairs. The sample in the photograph was made on satin, but it can also be reproduced on other materials, as for example cloth, velvet or moire, provided that it has sufficient body.

The design is to be traced in accordance with General Instructions. Machine to be prepared with Embroidery Thread No. 60 in the bobbin and needle No. 9, threaded with silk thread No. 00. The upper tension to be moderate and the bobbin tension a little tight.

Take a line of stitching around the outline and then a second line to reinforce the first, always using the lightest shade corresponding with each section. Then divide crosswise the interior of the petals in equal parts of $\frac{1}{8}$ of an inch. Beginning with the lightest shade, take a line of stitching and another line to reinforce, following the dividing line of the first part. Then fill this part with long stitches and finish it with raised and flat embroidery stitches. The balance of the sections of the entire flower are made in the same manner until all of the sections requiring that shade have been completed.

Then between each section make small groups of stitches on top of each other and in a straight line with the same shade of thread with which the corresponding section was made. Now change the thread and thread needle with the next darker shade, making all sections that call for this color, and then again change the silk and make the last sections with the darkest shade.

Embroider the leaves and the stems, following the same method as that for the flowers with the exception that green shades are to be used.

Lastly cover the outlines with chenille of a color that harmonizes with those used. Fasten this chenille with cross stitches at a distance of not more than $\frac{1}{4}$ to $\frac{1}{3}$ of an inch inch in the straight lines and $\frac{1}{8}$ to $\frac{1}{7}$ of an inch in the curves.

The center is done with silk in a manner similar to that explained in Lesson 21 ("Smyrna Embroidery"), the only difference being that in this case it should not be cut out.

MATERIAL: Satin.
THREADS: In the bobbin, Embroidery No. 60.
In the needle, Silk No. 00.
NEEDLE: No. 9.
TENSIONS: The upper tension moderate and the bobbin tension a little tight.

Imitation Velvet Embroidery

THIS is particularly adapted for cushions, upholstery, etc. When working on fine materials such as taffeta, satin, etc., some other thin material should be used as a reinforcement and should be applied on the wrong side. This reinforcement is not required when working on heavy fabrics such as moire or upholstery satin.

Prepare the machine with Embroidery Thread No. 60 in the bobbin and needle No. 9, same to be threaded with silk thread No. 00. The upper tension should be moderate and the bobbin tension a little tight.

After placing the material, which in this case is satin, into the hoops, trace the design as indicated in General Instructions and make

a line of stitching around the outline of the design.

Two heavy needles are required, which for convenience will be known as "A" and "B". Needles of other sizes may be used, according to the kind of work to be made.

Begin with needle "A" which temporarily serves as a filler, and work in the same way as when cording; that is to say, taking stitches crosswise, over the needle. Then place needle "B" close to needle "A" and cover it in the same manner. Draw needle "A", place it side by side of needle "B" and repeat the work until the leaf has been finished. The colors of the silk must be changed gradually so as to properly follow the pattern.

After the work has been concluded and before removing it from the hoops, apply on the wrong side a solution of gum and after it has dried, cut with very fine and sharp scissors through the center of the cording. This will produce a beautiful imitation of velvet.

MATERIAL: Upholstery Satin.

THREADS: In the bobbin, Embroidery No. 60. In the needle, Silk No. 00.

NEEDLE: No. 9.

TENSIONS: The upper tension moderate and the bobbin tension a little tight.

SINGER

INSTRUCTIONS

FOR

ART EMBROIDERY

AND

LACE WORK

THIRD COURSE

OF

STUDY

▽▽

SINGER SEWING MACHINE COMPANY

Crochet Lace

THE main features of this variety of lace are its smoothness and flexibility, which render it especially appropriate for the trimming of feminine undergarments.

The machine is to be prepared with Embroidery Thread No. 60 in the bobbin, needle No. 8 which should be threaded with Embroidery Thread No. 80. The upper tension should be moderate and the bobbin tension a little tight.

Insert organdie in the hoops, draw the design and baste Minardis (Picot Braid) with a zig-zag line of stitching which must be taken on the outline but taking care not to pierce the loops.

Begin with the sections where the tapering

bars are made, starting with the larger ones. Cut out as much material as may be required to make a bar and make a line of stitching, commencing at the center of the circle and reaching the loop where it is fastened. Draw from the machine a single thread to be used as a filler and cord the line of stitching with as many stitches as required. These stitches must be close together and on top of each other in the heavier parts of bar and gradually decreasing in number when getting to the final part of the bar, so as to obtain a tapering shape. Then cut out another piece of material and make the next tapering bar. Continue in the same way until all of the bars have been finished. Now cut the material from the interior of the circle and cord it with a strand of thread from the machine.

The connecting bars and the zig-zag in the background are made as explained in Lesson 13 ("English Lace"), but bear in mind that in this kind of lace all the bars must start from the loops of one of the edges and must finish at the corresponding loops on the other edge of the braid.

After the work has been finished and before removing it from the hoops, take out the bastings from the wrong side and leave no threads.

MATERIAL: Organdie.

BRAID: Minardis (Picot Braid).

THREADS: In the bobbin, Embroidery No. 60. In the needle, Embroidery No. 80.

NEEDLE: No. 8.

TENSIONS: The upper tension moderate and the bobbin tension a little tight.

Duchess Lace

THIS lace is a combination of small flowers or fancy stitches connected with curves which give the impression of stems. It is appropriate for use on bed spreads, cushions, handkerchief cases, etc.

Prepare the machine with Embroidery Thread No. 80 in the bobbin and needle No. 7, threaded with Embroidery Thread No. 100.

As a base use net of a round and small mesh.

For the stitching over the braid and the points on the net, both tensions must be moderate and even; for the cording, the tiny eyelets in the braid and for the background, the upper tension should be moderate and the bobbin tension a little tight.

After the design has been traced, take a

line of stitching around the outline and make the small eyelets in the center of the braid, cording the meshes. The eyelets must be located exactly in the center of the lines of stitching which mark the braid. Leave a little space between each of these eyelets (see Letter "A").

Section "B"—Is made by cording the meshes which were not worked between the eyelets. This is done on both sides of the row of eyelets. Then return to the space that was left between two of the eyelets and cord the meshes on both sides. Continue forward and cord another mesh in the same way as the two previously corded, thus forming a small buttonhole, and repeat the work that was made between the two previous meshes. The entire section is embroidered in the same manner.

Take five lines of stitching on each side of the eyelets so as to darn the braid.

Then make the points on the net, beginning with "C". These are worked in a direction opposite to that of the thread of the mesh by making a line of stitching over the outline of one mesh so as to form a tiny eyelet. Continue with the same line of stitching, cording the thread next to the eyelet, then continue over the outline of the next mesh and so on until the entire row has been completed. Skip one row of meshes and at the next repeat the operation until completing that row. Then take a line of stitching in an opposite direction crossing the eyelets made.

Letter "D"—Skip a row and repeat the operation until the entire section has been completed, but taking care that the closed meshes of one row correspond with those that were left open in the previous row; that is to say, alternating the closed meshes of one row with the open meshes of the next.

After the points on the net have been made, do the small lace darning similar to that of the Battenberg Embroidery (Lessons 31), and then the background as per instructions in Lesson 36 ("Fancy Lace"). Now make the bars in zig-zag as per explanation in Lesson 13 ("English Lace"), and immediately afterward make the bars with small darning points. These darning points should not exceed one-third the length of the bars.

The lace is finished by cording the entire outline with Irish Thread No. 80.

MATERIAL: Net with a round and small mesh.

THREADS: In the bobbin, Embroidery No. 80. In the needle, Embroidery No. 100. For the cording, Irish Thread No. 80.

NEEDLE: No. 7.

TENSIONS: For stitching on the braid and for the points on the net, both moderate and even. For cording, eyelets and the background, the upper tension should be moderate and the bobbin tension a little tight.

Bruges Lace

ITS fineness and beauty render this lace very appropriate for the ornamentation of altar cloths, albas and innumerable other uses such as bed spreads, curtains, etc.

The machine is prepared with Embroidery Thread No. 80 in the bobbin and in the needle. Use needle No. 8. The upper ten-sion should be moderate and the bobbin tension a little tight.

To reproduce work illustrated, net with a small round mesh must be used and braids, leaves and point lace of suitable sizes and designs.

Insert the net into the hoops and trace the

design as explained in Lesson 14 ("Brussels Lace"). Begin by applying the small leaves as described in said lesson; then make the lace and the small bars in the center of the flowers.

Proceed in a similar manner to apply the braid; then make the lace work as per letter "A", and make the corded lines of stitching with simple picot edging.

Now make the little bars which join the leaves with each other (Letter "B") and continue with those which join the braid with the lace as indicated in "C". These are similar to those explained in Lesson 36 ("Fancy Lace").

Finally remove the bastings from the wrong side of the work.

Remember that this lace should be made on organdie when it is intended for application on another piece of work and when such is not the case, as in the sample shown in the photograph, the net is to be used as a base only.

MATERIAL: Net with a round and small mesh.
BRAIDS: Leaves and Point Lace of an appropriate size.
THREADS: Embroidery No. 80 both in the bobbin and in the needle.
NEEDLE: No. 8.
TENSIONS: The upper tension moderate and the bobbin tension a little tight.

Spanish Point Lace

THIS is a solid and attractive variety of embroidery and is suitable for table cloths, cushions, curtains and for many other similar purposes.

The machine is prepared with Embroidery Thread No. 80 in the bobbin and in the needle. Needle No. 8. The upper tension should be moderate and the bobbin tension a little tighter.

As a base use organdie on which the design should be traced, then take a line of stitching around the outline and reinforce it using a single thread from the machine as a filler.

Use a filler of two double strands of darning cotton to reinforce the lines of stitching already made and begin to make the little bars which separate the larger circles ("A"), cutting the material out little by little as you proceed.

Then make the zig-zag lines of stitching in the center, afterward those next and then the bars as per letter "B", finishing with other zig-zag lines.

Finally make the braid with buttonhole stitch on both sides, carrying as a filler a single strand of darning cotton on each side.

If the lace is to be applied on another piece of work, do not reinforce the exterior outline until after it has been basted on the material, when you may proceed to cord, finishing by making the braid with buttonhole stitch on both sides.

MATERIAL: Organdies.

THREADS: Embroidery No. 80 in the bobbin and in the needle.

For the guides, darning cotton.

NEEDLE: No. 8.

TENSIONS: The upper tension moderate and the lower tension a little tight.

Genoese Net

THIS lace is very useful for table runners, shades, etc., it can also be used as applique or for insertions and lace.

Prepare the machine with Embroidery Thread No. 80 in the bobbin and in the needle. Use Needle No. 8. For the cording, double stitching and buttonhole stitch, upper tension moderate, bobbin tension a little tight; for the meshes and the stitching both should be moderate and even.

As a base use organdie on which the outlines of the square should be traced.

Then take a line of stitching and reinforce it, carrying as a filler a single thread from

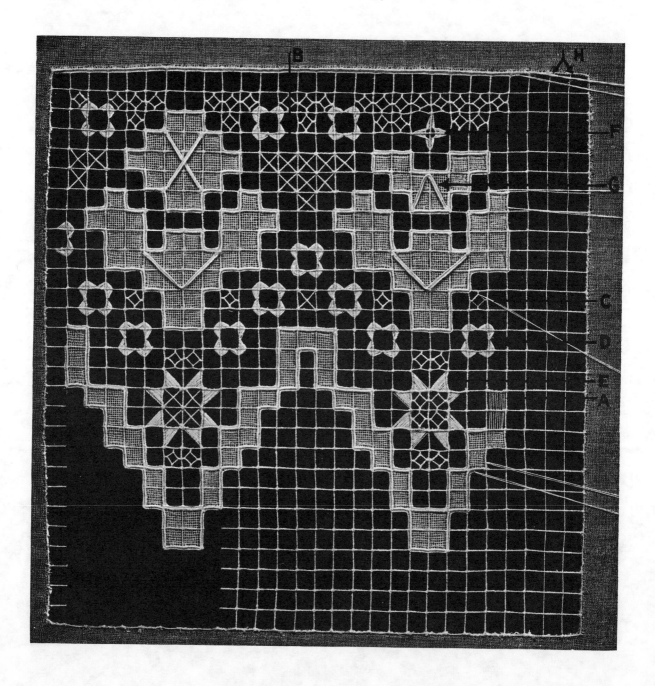

the machine. Keep before you the model or design so as to take exactly the correct number of meshes required.

Change the thread, inserting No. 200 both in the needle and in the bobbin and do the meshes, following instructions given in Lesson 15 "Filet Lace". Then again insert Embroidery Thread No. 80, draw a single thread from the machine and neatly cord the meshes, taking nine stitches at each crossing so as to form a little knot. Now you may proceed with the different darning stitches and other trimmings shown in the photograph.

Point "A"—This point is made as a darning of the Filet Lace. It can be made in combination with Point "G".

Point "B"—Take a line of stitching in a zig-zag, repeat in an opposite direction, then draw a double strand of thread from the machine and cord both lines.

Point "C"—The little diamond is made as per explanations given in Lesson 29, "Hedebo Embroidery", Point "D", with which the "Spirit Point" is produced.

Point "D"—At each corner of the center mesh, make a darning stitch over the four threads; take a stitch at each space and go over the work several times until the design is reproduced exactly.

Point "E"—For this Point and for Point "F" use embroidery thread No. 60 both in the needle and in the bobbin and needle No. 9. Take lines of running stitches parallel to each other and in a diagonal direction, starting from the corners. Take one stitch in the center mesh and two stitches in the mesh where the diagonal line is fastened so that all the threads are properly secured.

Point "F"—Make a line of stitches over the four threads of the center point of four meshes forming a small circle, then start from this circle and make similar lines of stitches to those which make up Point "E".

Point "G"—This consists of a small bar of double stitching, and is made without the use of hoops. Carry a double strand of Irish Thread with a knitting needle or with the point of the scissors and make a double line of cording, applying wherever the design calls for it.

After making the ornamental points baste a single thread of darning cotton over the outline of the darning, Point "A", and with a double strand of thread from the machine make the buttonhole stitching. See the photograph.

In the case of lace points as that reproduced in the photograph, the work is to be finished with buttonhole stitching over all the outside outline and then the ends of the mesh threads are to be neatly cut in such parts where no work has been done. To add any other parts that may be made subsequently, leave two threads uncorded on one side of the meshes. ("H").

Now change the position of the material in the hoops so as to include in the hoops five rows of meshes, more or less, and again trace the design, pass the vertical threads on the side opposite that which has already been worked and cross the horizontal threads which are a continuation of those left without reinforcement ("H"), cutting it when getting to the other end.

Now make the reinforcement of the meshes and the several ornamental points in the same manner as previously done.

MATERIAL: Organdie.

THREADS: For the meshes Sewing Thread No. 200 in the bobbin and in the needle.
For the cording and ornamental stitches, except Points "E" and "F", Embroidery No. 80 both in the bobbin and in the needle. For Points "E" and "F" Embroidery No. 60 at both places. For Point "G" Irish Thread No. 70.

NEEDLES: No. 8 for Threads Nos. 80 and 200 No. 9 for Thread No. 60.

TENSIONS: For the cording, the double stitch and the buttonhole stitch, the upper tension moderate and the bobbin tension a little tight; for the meshes and the stitching both moderate and even.

Malta Lace

THIS lace is delicate and simple and is a favorite with ladies of good taste. The distinctive feature is the Malta Cross; this Cross should always serve as the outstanding feature of the design.

Prepare the machine with Embroidery Thread No. 80 in the bobbin and Needle No. 7 which should be threaded with the same class of thread but No. 100. As a base, use organdie on which the design should be traced.

Both tensions should be moderate and even for the darning point and for the little Bone Lace Leaves, but for the bars and the cording the upper tension should be moderate and the bobbin tension a little tight.

Take a line of stitching for the outline of

the design, draw a single strand of thread from the machine and reinforce neatly. Begin with the small triangles in the center, making them with Darning Stitch (Lesson No. 45, "Bone Lace Insertions") and continue with the balance of the figure and the little leaves with the same stitch.

Make the little bars as explained in Lesson 29, "Hedebo Embroidery", and then make the small leaves of Bone Lace as per instructions in Lesson 17, "Bone Lace—First Applique".

The background is finished by making the bars to join the several sections of the work; these bars are produced as explained in Lesson No. 13 "English Lace".

Carry a strand of Irish Thread No. 80 and cord the outline of the interior and conclude by making the small points around the outline as indicated in the photograph. Cut out the material from the interior of these points and then cord them, also cord the outline which serves as the base of the points.

MATERIAL: Organdie.
THREADS: In the bobbin, Embroidery No. 80. In the needle, Embroidery No. 100. For the cording, Irish Thread No. 80.
NEEDLE: No. 7.
TENSIONS: For the darning and the little Bone Lace Leaves both moderate and even; for the Bars and Cording the upper moderate and the bobbin tension somewhat tight.

Bone Lace Edging

AFTER having mastered Bone Lace—First Applique, as per Lesson No. 17 and Bone Lace Insertions as explained in Lesson No. 45, we may try this other variety of Bone Lace which is called "Edging" and which is, of course, somewhat more complicated and of great artistic value. It is used in many shapes and sizes. The narrow strips of Edging are appropriate for underwear, the wide ones for table linen, bed linen and similar purposes, while the middle sizes are applicable to a great variety of purposes.

Prepare the machine with Embroidery Thread No. 80 in the bobbin and Needle

No. 7 which should be threaded with Embroidery Thread No. 100. For the stitching and the lace points both tensions are to be moderate and even; for the balance of the work the upper tension moderate and the bobbin tension a little tight.

Use as a base organdie on which the design is to be traced, then take a line of stitching around the outline and neatly reinforce with a filling of single thread taken from the machine.

Begin by doing the Darning Stitch in the smaller sections, following directions contained in Lesson 45, then proceed with those sections which are done with "Half Stitch" in accordance with instructions given in the above mentioned lesson. Continue over the upper edge and gradually cut out the material between the two parallel lines of stitching and take vertical stitches close to each other from one side to the other, making the two groups of darning which can be seen in the photograph. Each one of these groups has six turns.

Then cut out the interior of the small scallops at the upper edge and draw a double strand of thread from the machine to serve as a filler in making the buttonhole stitch.

Afterward with a buttonhole stitch make the little bars which complete the circles made with the darning stitch and continue with the small Bone Lace Leaves connecting the sections already finished ("A"). Proceed with the bars in the background, taking care not to make those that join the Bone Lace Leaves, as they are to be made in one operation "B" as explained in Lesson No. 17—Point "I".

Now make the Bone Lace Leaves which are superimposed on the circles of darning. To do this use another set of hoops, insert a piece of organdie, trace a circle of the proper size and make the required leaves. Then cut these out and apply them on the work for which they are intended.

To make the scallops at the lower edge, cut out the material from the interior of each and apply a strand of darning cotton and another strand of Irish Thread No. 80 and do the buttonhole stitch, bearing in mind that in each scallop three tiny loops are to be made, as may be seen in the photograph.

The scallops on the upper edge are made by cutting out the material from the interior of each and doing the buttonhole stitch. For this purpose a double strand of thread from the machine is used as a filler.

To conclude, baste the outline with a strand of darning cotton and then make the buttonhole stitch, using as a filler a double thread from the machine.

The small scallops on both edges may also be made, if desired, in the manner similar to that described in Lesson 26 "Teneriffe Wheels".

MATERIAL: Organdie.
THREADS: In the bobbin, Embroidery No. 80.
In the needle, Embroidery No. 100.
For the Scallops—Irish Thread No. 80.
For the outlines and scallops—darning cotton.
NEEDLE: No. 7.
TENSIONS: For the stitching on lace work, both moderate and even; for the balance of the work the upper tension moderate and the bobbin tension a little tight.

Guipiur Lace

THE sample reproduced in the photograph is a beautiful pattern of Guipiur Lace. This variety of lace is a combination of several artistic points and lends itself for the trimming of innumerable feminine garments and also for many uses in the home.

The machine is prepared with Embroidery Thread No. 60 in the bobbin and Embroidery Thread No. 80 in the needle. Needle No. 8.

In making the Raised Embroidery and the background, both tensions should be moderate and even; for the double cording the upper tension moderate and the bobbin tension somewhat tight.

As a base use organdie on which the design should be traced. Then take a line of stitching around the outline and reinforce with a filler of thread from the machine.

The raised embroidery for the little leaves and eyelets is made by filling in the space with stitches. In the leaves the stitches should be taken lengthwise and then crosswise or in the same direction as the raised embroidery.

After the raised embroidery has been completed, begin with the background of the lace.

Sections similar to "A" are produced by following directions contained in Lesson 36, "Fancy Lace", with the exception that the little picot edges are made by taking four successive stitches from the edge of the filler and without cording. This produces tiny loops.

Sections such as "B" are made by forming a background of meshes, slightly reinforce, then make tiny loops in the same way as indicated in connection with "A".

When the background has been completed make the raised embroidery on the leaves and eyelets which have already been prepared. Cut out the material between the leaves and join them. (Study Photograph). Then make the double cording as indicated in "C", carrying as a filler on each side a double strand of thread from the machine.

Finally do the edges and make parallel lines of stitching slightly reinforced. Then finish the interior and exterior of these edges with a double line of cording.

MATERIAL: Organdie.

THREADS: In the bobbin, Embroidery No. 60.
In the needle, Embroidery No. 80.

NEEDLE: No. 8.

TENSIONS: For the preparation of the raised embroidery in the background both moderate and even; for the double cording, the upper tension moderate and the bobbin tension a little tight.

Venetian Lace

THIS delicate style of embroidery is always in fashion. It can be applied with the most beautiful effect on fans, handkerchiefs, etc.

Organdie should be used as a base. Prepare the machine with Embroidery Thread No. 80 in the bobbin, and Needle No. 7 threaded with Embroidery Thread No. 100.

For the different lace points and darning both tensions are to be moderate and even. For the "Venetian Half Stitch" the bobbin tension should be tight and the upper tension not quite so tight; for the cording and the background the upper tension moderate and the bobbin tension somewhat tight.

After tracing the design, take a line of stitching around the entire outline and

reinforce with a filler of thread from the machine; then begin with the sections which require the darning stitch, doing first the large sections and then the others. Continue with the several lace points, the execution of which is similar to that which was explained in Lessons 41 and 42, "Renaissance Lace".

Now make the section with "Half Stitch" as instructed in Lesson 33, "Blond Lace", and continue with the little leaves which are to be made with Venetian Half Stitch (Lessons 22 and 23, "Venetian Lace") and which should be combined with darning stitch in the the narrower parts.

The hemstitching which forms the edges on the sides is made by stitching crosswise in the same manner as is done with the darning stitch, then take another line of stitching which will cross the lines at their center, forming in this way little groups of three threads each.

The lace work in the background is made in accordance with instructions contained in Lesson 36, "Fancy Lace".

Afterward make the lace points in the empty spaces of the sections that have been worked with darning stitch and then make the tapering bars of the lower circle which are the same as those described in Lesson 51, "Crochet Lace", and they also have the little picot effect which was dealt with in Lesson 16, "Milan Lace".

The work is completed by making buttonholes as indicated in the photograph and by completing the part of the background that was left undone. Finally cord the outlines with a filler of Irish Thread No. 80.

MATERIAL: Organdie.
THREADS: In the bobbin, Embroidery No. 80.
In the needle, Embroidery No. 100
For the outlines Irish Thread No. 80.
NEEDLE: No. 7.
TENSIONS: For the lace points and the darning both moderate and even; for the Venetian Half Stitch the bobbin tension tight, the upper tension somewhat less tight; for the background and cording the upper tension moderate and the bobbin tension a little tighter.

Venetian Lace—Faces and Figures

VENETIAN LACE, the first points of which were explained in Lessons 22 and 23, is as a rule selected for pieces of work where faces or figures are shown, as this particular style of lace work is most suitable for this purpose.

Prepare the machine with Embroidery Thread No. 80 in the bobbin and Needle No. 7, which should be threaded with Embroidery Thread No. 100. As a base use organdie. For the Venetian Half Stitch the bobbin tension should be tight and the upper tension

FIGURE 1

somewhat less tight; for the other points the bobbin tension should be somewhat tight and the upper tension moderate.

It is very important to trace the design on the material in great detail, taking care that the threads of the organdie which cross

FIGURE 2

vertically are in a straight line on the features of the face or on the body of the figure. If the profile is not neat and of good proportions the lace will lose much of its merit and attraction.

FACES

Take the usual lines of stitching and cut out a piece of material from the most salient point; that is to say, the nose, and begin the Venetian Half Stitch, "Lessons 22 and 23 Point "A"), continue with the balance until the entire face has been completed as may be seen in the photograph. Then make the eyebrow and the eye with a small cord. The hair is made with a very close stitch (Lessons 22 and 23, Point "B") and finish with small bars as a sort of ornamentation.

Proceeding with the dress, the collar should be made with triangular stitch (Lessons 22 and 23, Point "C") and finished with buttonhole stitch so that the blouse stands out. The blouse is embroidered with Point "D" of the above mentioned Lessons.

On the line dividing the Venetian Half Stitch from the triangular point, a zig-zag line is to be made. For the hair and the dress, any one of the points described in Lessons Nos. 22 and 23 may be utilized as they are all suitable for this kind of work.

After completing all the Venetian points shown in the photograph, make the background. Take a line of stitching over the hexagons and reinforce it; cut out the material from the interior and again reinforce the stitching with a strand of thread from the machine and make the buttonhole stitch. To conclude, cord the profile of the face and make a small raised stitching on the lips, taking care to preserve the proper proportion, and then do buttonhole stitching over the balance of the outline.

FIGURES

The method to be followed in making figures is the same as already explained in connection with faces. The operator may choose the points according to her taste, except with regard to faces and uncovered parts of the body, which in every case are to be made with the Venetian Half Stitch.

As may be observed in the lower part of the figure shown in the photograph, there is a new stitch which is based on the Venetian Half Stitch with slight variations. This point is made as follows:

In the first row make eight small bars of Venetian Half Stitch and leave a space of about $1/25$ inch, again make another eight bars and leave another similar empty space, and continue in the same way until reaching the end of the row at which point, after turning the hoops, begin with the second row.

In the second row make six little bars and leave a space of about $1/25$ inch, then make two bars and again leave a space of $1/25$ inch, then make six bars and repeat in this way until the end of the row.

On the next row leave similar spaces between each eight bars. Care is to be taken that the two small bars that are made in the second row are exactly under the empty space of the first row and above the empty space of the third row.

In making the next three rows, change the order of the bars and the space in such a way that the empty spaces are not placed under the previous empty spaces but in between them. With this combination of bars and spaces an attractive style of embroidery is produced and it may be changed to suit the taste of the operator simply by changing the distances.

With similar variations a great number of different points may be made, but one must always bear in mind that the Venetian points only should be used.

MATERIAL: Organdie.
THREADS: In the bobbin, Embroidery No. 80.
            In the needle, Embroidery No. 100.
NEEDLE: No. 7.
TENSIONS: For the Venetian Half Stitch the bobbin tension tight and the upper tension not so tight.
            For the balance of the work the bobbin tension a little tight and the needle tension moderate.

Cross Stitch

THE beauty and usefulness of this Point were discovered by the head of the Singer Embroidery Academy in Santiago, Republic of Chile, South America. It is very attractive because it is in colors and also on account of its design.

The machine is prepared by winding on the bobbin Embroidery Thread No. 60 and threading the needle with Embroidery Silk No. 00 of an appropriate color. Needle No. 9.

The upper tension should be moderate and the bobbin tension somewhat tight.

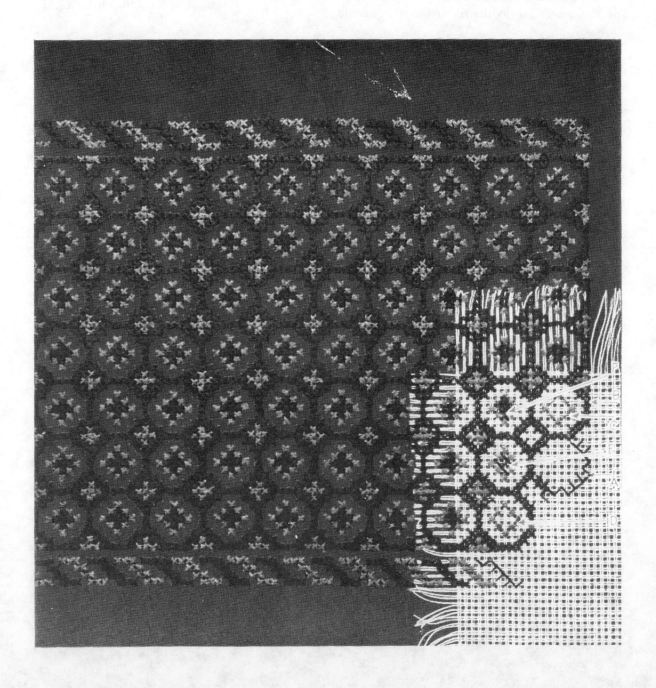

Insert in the hoops the material selected which may be either thin or heavy, in this case "Mongol Crepe" has been used.

Baste on the material canvas of small meshes and count the meshes when doing the work, so as to be able to exactly reproduce the pattern. Begin with the background, using colored silk, and take small stitches in a diagonal direction, starting at the center of one mesh and reaching to the next, following the lines of the pattern (see "A"). Make one row in this manner and then over it make the stitches in the shape of a cross as will be seen at "B".

Then make the small squares in the center of the row. To do these, thread the needle with blue silk and make the small square at "C"; then complete it as may be seen at "D".

Change the silk to red and do the center of the square as may be seen at "E" and finish as indicated at "F".

Lastly make the border as has already been explained and then carefully remove the canvas which was used to follow the pattern.

MATERIALS: Mongol Crepe, canvas of small mesh.
THREADS: In the bobbin, Embroidery No. 60. In the needle, Sewing Silk No. 00.
NEEDLE: No. 9.
TENSIONS: The upper tension moderate and the bobbin tension a little tight.

Raised Embroidery on Mesh

THIS is an attractive combination of raised embroidery and Filet Lace and on account of its firmness and simplicity it is of great value for trimming of curtains, shades, white goods and table linen in general.

The machine should be prepared for making the mesh as indicated in Lesson 15, "Filet Lace", and for making the raised embroidery in accordance with instructions in Lesson 8, "Scalloping and Raised Embroidery—Satin Stitch". The tensions are to be the same as indicated in the above mentioned Lessons.

First make the meshes and then trace the design for the raised embroidery on a piece

of organdie which is to be applied on the mesh. After this make the filling as was explained in Lesson 8. Then cut out the organdie and apply on the wrong side a piece of transparent and stiff paper as a reinforcement and make the raised embroidery. After the work has been completed carefully remove any pieces of paper that may have remained.

MATERIAL: Organdie.

THREADS: For the meshes sewing thread No. 200 both in the bobbin and in the needle.

For the cording Embroidery Thread, No. 60 in the bobbin and No. 80 in the needle.

For the raised embroidery, Embroidery Thread No. 80 in the bobbin and No. 60 in the needle.

NEEDLE: For the meshes No. 8.

For the raised embroidery No. 9.

TENSIONS: For the meshes, both moderate and even.

For the cording and raised embroidery, upper tension moderate and the bobbin tension a little tight.

Embroidery With Gold or Silver Thread
AND
Persian Embroidery

THIS is an odd and artistic combination of embroidery. It is used as fancy work by itself or combined with others, as may be seen in the sample reproduced. A very attractive effect may be obtained by combining it with "Rococo Embroidery" (Lesson 48).

It can be produced on many varieties of material, either transparent or of very close weave, such as washable silk, cotton crepe, satin, tulle, charmeuse, etc. The sample reproduced in the photograph was made on charmeuse.

The design should be traced, at the same time, on both sides of the material. For this purpose, two sheets of carbon paper should be utilized, placing one, in the usual manner, over the material and under the design, and the other one under the wrong side of the material with the tracing face against the fabric. In this way the design will be reproduced on both sides.

EMBROIDERY WITH GOLD OR SILVER THREAD

Prepare the machine with fine metallic thread in the bobbin and leave the tension loose enough to permit the thread to go through without twisting; use Needle No. 9 which should be threaded with sewing silk No. 00 of the same color as that of the metallic thread. The tension of the needle should be somewhat tighter than that of the bobbin.

Insert the material in the hoops face downward. Begin with embroidery stitches, which should be somewhat long and uniform and at the same time they must be close together and parallel with each other. Cover the lines of the design, being careful to carry the hoops forward. The embroidery will appear on the right side of the material, which is the under side.

After finishing the part which is to be embroidered with metallic thread, remove the material from the hoops and again insert it in the hoops, but this time face upward, that is to say, in the usual way. The material being placed in this position, you can now proceed with the

PERSIAN EMBROIDERY

Select seven (7) colors of silk sewing No. 00, of vivid and different shades. These silks are wound together, by hand, on the bobbin, filling the bobbin a little over half and endeavoring to have the threads wound evenly, as this is essential. After inserting the bobbin in the bobbin case, have the seven (7) threads pass together under the tension spring, loosening the screw as much as possible.

Then insert No. 19 needle and thread it with silk of any one of the colors in the bobbin. The needle thread tension should be as tight as possible.

In taking the first stitch, the high tension of the upper thread will draw the seven (7) threads of the bobbin and cord them together. With the upper thread, begin with one of the edges and continue until the entire design has been covered with short and even stitches.

MATERIAL: Charmeuse.

THREADS: For the embroidery with gold or silver thread—in the bobbin, metallic thread. In the needle, sewing silk No. 00.
For the Persian Embroidery—in the bobbin, sewing silk No. 00 (7 different colors). In the needle, sewing silk No. 00.

NEEDLES: No. 9 for embroidery with gold or silver thread.
No. 19 for the Persian enbroidery

TENSIONS: For embroidery with gold or silver thread, bobbin tension loose; upper tension a little tight.
For the Persian embroidery, bobbin tension as loose as possible; upper tension as tight as the silk will stand.

Chinese Embroidery

THIS is one of the most beautiful and attractive styles of embroidery. The variety of coloring and the originality of its design reveal the country of origin. It is no longer required, however, to have as much patience, nor to take as long a time as the Chinese do in order to produce this wonderful work of art, as the perfect mechanism of the Singer machine permits its execution on shawls, cushions, piano covers, etc., with as much neatness and in a shorter time than when made by hand.

The materials appropriate for this work are crepe de chine, cotton crepe, satin and similar

fabrics. The machine is to be prepared in accordance with the fabric to be used. For very fine fabrics, such as crepe de chine or cotton crepe, sewing silk No.00 should be used, with the same color both in the bobbin and the needle, and needle No. 9. For such materials the upper tension should be moderate and the bobbin tension very tight, in order that the wrong side of the fabric will show almost as perfect a finish as that on the right side.

The sample shown in the photograph has been made on satin, using organdie on the wrong side as a reinforcement. The machine was prepared with embroidery thread No. 60 in the bobbin and No. 9 needle threaded with sewing silk No. 00 of an appropriate color. The upper tension should be moderate and the bobbin tension a little tight.

Make a line of stitching around the outline, using the desired color for each section. Begin by taking stitches on the bias over such parts as appear to be under others; in this case the stems and the leaves, except that marked "A", which is made afterwards, due to the fact that it covers a part of the bud.

Continue with the flowers, beginning with the outside line of petals and starting with the lightest shade. The stitches are to be very close together and perfectly even. After the first section has been finished, change the silk and thread the needle with the next shade of color. Take a line of stitches with this silk over the end of the section just completed, then neatly reinforce same, using a single strand of thread from the machine. (See "B"). Then proceed with the second section until finished, and afterwards successively change the shades in making the subsequent sections in the same way.

The center of the flower is made with long stitches very close together and, as a rule, using a color different from those already used. In this case the color used was blue.

It is important to bear in mind that in this class of embroidery the shades are not blended together but, on the contrary, each color must neatly stand out, always endeavoring to give them the effect of being placed on different surfaces.

MATERIALS: Satin.

Organdie as a reinforcement.

THREADS: For embroidery work on satin, embroidery thread No. 60 in the bobbin. In the needle silk thread No. 00. For embroidery on very fine materials, sewing silk No. 00 of the same color both in the bobbin and the needle.

NEEDLE: No. 9.

TENSIONS: For work on satin, the upper tension moderate and the bobbin tension a little tight.

For work on very fine fabrics, the upper tension moderate and the bobbin tension very tight.

Wool Embroidery on Net

THIS embroidery work is particularly suitable, on account of its firmness, for upholstery work of many varieties and, because of its beauty, can also be used to advantage in many combinations of other embroidery works.

Make the meshes, following the instructions given in Lesson No. 75, "Italian Filet", after having prepared the machine in accordance with instructions in the above mentioned lesson.

After all the meshes have been completed, make the darning stitch. Prepare the machine with wool a little twisted, and of the desired

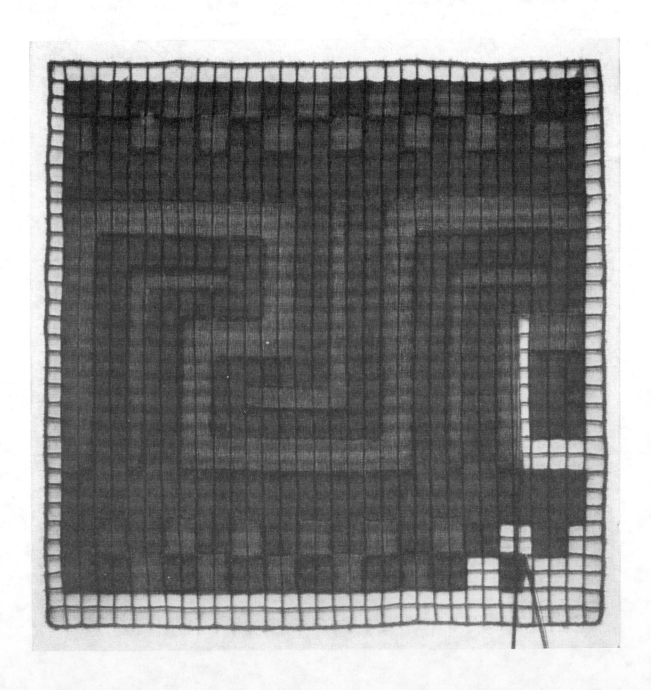

color, in the bobbin, and needle No. 9, which should be threaded with sewing silk No. 00 of the same shade as the wool. The bobbin tension is to be loose and that of the needle moderate.

The background of the darning here is dark red. The stitches are to be taken in a manner similar to that used in connection with the darning of "Italian Filet". Then change the wool in the bobbin and the silk in the needle, inserting blue wool and silk respectively, and make the sections that require this color.

It is advisable to select designs or patterns which, after covering all the meshes, will give the impression of a weave. Also bear in mind that the size of the meshes should never be smaller than indicated in the photograph, but rather larger.

MATERIALS: Organdie.

THREADS: For the stitching and reinforcement, black sewing silk No. 00 both in the bobbin and in the needle.

For the meshes, black sewing thread No. 100, both in the bobbin and the needle.

For the cording, black sewing thread No. 100 in the bobbin and black sewing silk No. 00 in the needle.

For the darning, fine twisted wool in the bobbin and in the needle sewing silk No. 00 of the same color as the wool.

NEEDLE: No. 9.

TENSIONS: For the stitching, reinforcement and the meshes, both moderate and even.

For cording the meshes, the upper tension moderate and the bobbin tension somewhat tight.

For the darning, the upper tension moderate and the bobbin tension loose.

Artistic Shaded Embroidery

A DESIRE to attempt to produce a piece of embroidery work similar to that shown in the photograph is ample proof that the operator has thoroughly mastered all the preceding lessons and that she is possessed of truly artistic inclinations. In this class of embroidery, she will find a good opportunity to develop her acquired knowledge and artistic taste.

The materials that may be used are satin, moire, cotton crepe or other similar fabrics. In the sample reproduced in the photograph satin was used.

The machine should be prepared with em-

broidery thread No. 60 in the bobbin, and needle No. 9, which should be threaded with sewing silk No. 00 of an appropriate shade. The upper tension must be moderate and the bobbin tension somewhat tight.

After the design has been traced, take a line of stitching and then over the first line take two more lines of stitches. Then begin with the artistic stitches, which must start from the edge of each section toward the interior. The colors are to be used following the pattern and taking alternately long and short stitches in an artistic way, also taking care that all of the stitches are taken exactly over the lines of stitching, so as to form a raised edge of neat finish.

The desired effect will be obtained by making groups of stitches. No particular size for these stitches can be suggested; it all depends upon the good taste and the ability of the operator. Some of the lines which divide the sections and others which serve as outline, are made diagonally to the line of stitching, that is to say, on the bias, in the same way as the stems described in Lessons 24 and 25—"Shaded Embroidery".

MATERIAL: Satin.
THREADS: In the bobbin, Embroidery No. 60.
In the needle, Sewing Silk No. 00.
NEEDLE: No. 9.
TENSIONS: The upper tension moderate.
The bobbin tension somewhat tight.

Granite Stitch—(Round Stitch)

THIS embroidery has characteristic features different from any of the varieties of embroidery already explained. There are no rules for the direction of the stitches nor for their shape, and the production of the work consists of making ordinary stitching of a minute size. This stitch is known as "Granite" or "Round Stitch".

Gauze, organdie, washable silk or some other similar fabric may be used. In tracing the design it is essential to show as much detail as possible, so as to be able to more easily give the coloring required. It is also advisable to keep the model or pattern before the operator so as to make a true reproduction.

The machine is to be prepared with em-

broidery thread No. 60 in the bobbin, and needle No. 9, which should be threaded with sewing silk No. 00 of the color desired. Both tensions are to be somewhat tight and even.

After taking a line of stitches around the outline, first do the sections that appear to be furthest away, so that the raised effect of the other sections may be nearer. The stitches must be very small and in the shape of small undulations, and they must be taken from the edge toward the interior, taking care not to make them too close together so that afterwards it will be possible to blend them with other colors. Each section is done in a similar way.

These stitches are simply ordinary stitches and their direction varies at the will of the operator, by moving the hoops, thus forming small undulations, which being mixed with each other, until all the material is covered, produce a granulated surface of flat coloring.

The appearance of a piece of embroidery made with this stitch will convince anyone of the fact that this "Granite" or "Round" stitch is by far the best adapted for the reproduction of pictures, combinations of flowers or fruits, and particularly for the imitation of persons, the sky or water.

In this work, the silk loses its luster and, for this reason, it is suitable to obtain the appearance desired. Also, it permits the blending of colors and obtaining softness in the several shades.

MATERIAL: Gauze.

THREADS: In the bobbin, Embroidery No. 60.
In the needle, Sewing Silk No. 00.

NEEDLE: No. 9.

TENSIONS: Both somewhat tight and even.

Penelope Embroidery

THIS variety of work is used for the ornamentation of cushions, piano covers and a great many other pieces of ornamental work. In the production of this embroidery, braid known as "Penelope" is used for the flowers; and for the stems and leaves, twisted artificial silk.

The machine is prepared with embroidery thread No. 60 in the bobbin, and needle No. 9, which is threaded with sewing silk No. 00 of an appropriate color. The upper tension must be moderate and the bobbin tension somewhat tight. The material to be used may be satin, moire or other similar fabrics.

The sample shown in the photograph was made on moire silk, on which the design was traced.

First the stems and leaves were made, and the bud was made after the petals were produced.

Take a line of stitching over the outline, then fasten a strand of artificial silk at the border of one leaf and carrying it in a diagonal direction toward the center, fasten it with one stitch and again return to the edge. Repeat this operation, following the direction of the design and properly shading until the leaf has been completed. Then apply a strand of silk of an appropriate color to form the vein.

The stems are also made with strands of artificial silk, but stitching on the bias. Fasten the strands with one stitch at the end of the stem and cross it in diagonal direction until reaching the opposite border where it should be secured with another stitch, and continue in this way to the end. First make the small stems, being careful to properly cover their union with the larger stems.

Then make the flowers and the bud. Remove the basting from one side of the braid but keep it on the other side which is used for its application and secure the braid gradually on the rim of the circle which indicates the outside of the petals, and continue turning toward the interior of the flower. Leave in the center a little space where the pistils should be formed. These are made following instructions in Lesson No. 21—"Smyrna Embroidery", but using in this case sewing silk.

The bud is made in a similar manner, making as many turns as the design may call for, in this case one and a half turns, and is finished by making the calyx with artificial silk. This should be done in the same way as the leaves and being careful to thoroughly cover the extreme end of the braid. The flowers may be shaded as shown in the photograph by using alternately the several colors of braid so as to properly follow the shading of the pattern. This change of colors is usually made at every two turns.

MATERIAL: Moire Silk.
  BRAID: Penelope.
THREADS: In the bobbin, Embroidery No. 60. In the needle, Sewing Silk No. 00, Twisted Artificial Silk.
NEEDLE: No. 9.
TENSIONS: The upper tension moderate. The bobbin tension somewhat tight.

Shaded Embroidery on Velvet or Plush

THIS embroidery is used for cushions, table covers and all kinds of tapestry or fancy pieces of work.

The design should be traced on organdie, which is placed over the velvet and on the wrong side of the velvet another piece of organdie is applied as a reinforcement. Then the work is inserted in the hoops.

The machine is prepared with embroidery thread No. 60 and needle No. 9, which is threaded with sewing silk No. 00 of the desired color.

The upper tension should be moderate and the bobbin tension a little tight.

Take a line of stitching over the outline and then another to reinforce the first, and

cut out the organdie around the outside. Study the photograph, then make shaded embroidery, following instructions contained in Lessons 24 and 25—"Shaded Embroidery", but leaving undone the parts of the petals which appear raised. These are made after the shading has been finished and by following directions given in Lesson 50—"Imitation Velvet Embroidery", using the color of silk that may be required.

After the work has been finished it should be ironed on the wrong side and again ironed after it has been removed from the hoops. Great care has to be taken in both cases so as to avoid marring the velvet.

MATERIALS: Velvet.

Organdie.

THREADS: In the bobbin, Embroidery No. 60.

In the needle, Sewing Silk No. 00.

NEEDLE: No. 9.

TENSIONS: Upper tension moderate.

Bobbin tension somewhat tight.

Italian Filet

THIS lace may be used on sofa cushions, curtains, table runners, etc. Due to the fact that it may be made with a great variety of shades, both in the net itself and in the darning, the usefulness of this work is practically unlimited.

The machine is to be prepared by winding black sewing silk No. 00 in the bobbin and using needle No. 9, which should be threaded with silk of the same class and number. Both tensions are to be moderate and even.

As a base use organdie or some other similar material on which the square for the net should be traced; then indicate with

small lines on the edge of the material, in each direction, the lines that are to be made. Take a line of stitching over the outline of the square and neatly reinforce with a single strand of thread from the machine which will be used as a filler.

For the meshes use black sewing thread No. 100 in the bobbin and in the needle instead of silk, and continue following the instructions given in Lesson 15 "Filet Lace".

After all the meshes have been made change the upper thread, inserting black sewing silk No. 00, tighten the bobbin tension a little, leaving the upper tension moderate, and cord carrying as a filler a single thread from the machine. Take seven stitches at each crossing to form the little knots.

For the darning change the threads, inserting in the bobbin and in the needle, sewing silk No. 00 of an appropriate color. Begin with one section, shown as "A" and do the first shade which should be the lightest and then the second. Proceed in the same way with subsequent meshes and gradually modify the shades until the section has been finished, then do the next section in an identical way. The darning is the same as the hemstitching and is made by taking one stitch only between each mesh. Then apply on the edge of the darning two strands of plain artificial silk of a color similar to those used in different sections. In applying these strands of silk take long stitches and twist the strands as they are being applied so that the stitches that are being taken in fastening them will not be seen after the work is finished.

MATERIAL: Organdie.

THREADS: For the stitching and reinforcements, Black Sewing Silk No. 00 in the needle and in the bobbin; for the meshes, Black Sewing Thread No. 100 in the bobbin and in the needle; for the cording, Black Sewing Silk No. 00 in the needle and Black Sewing Thread No. 100 in the bobbin. For the darning, Sewing Silk No. 00 of an appropriate color in the needle and in the bobbin.

For the edge of the darning, plain artificial silk.

NEEDLE: No. 9.

TENSIONS: For the stitching, reinforcement and meshes, both moderate and even; for the cording and darning, the upper tension moderate and the bobbin tension a little tight.

SINGER

INSTRUCTIONS

FOR

ART EMBROIDERY

AND

LACE WORK

FOURTH COURSE

OF

STUDY

▼▼

SINGER SEWING MACHINE COMPANY

Frivolite Lace

THE distinguishing feature of this lace is its originality; but in order to obtain the delicate effect which this work calls for, suitable attention must be taken in its execution.

Prepare the machine with Embroidery Thread No. 80 in the bobbin, needle No. 8 and thread of the same class and number in the needle. Both tensions should be somewhat tight and even.

As a base use organdie on which the design should be traced in the usual way and begin with a line of stitching over the outline, which should be carefully and neatly reinforced

with a strand of thread from the machine.

Cut out the material from the interior of one section at a time to prevent the design from losing its shape, and join the several parts with lines of stitches as you proceed with the work. Cut out the interior of the loops in the center of the section and make on them buttonhole stitching, for which purpose a double strand of thread from the machine must be basted and carried as a filler and another strand of thread with which the tiny loops on the exterior are made. (Consult the photograph).

The exterior of each section is made in the same way, cutting out the material on the outside and fastening and joining the different sections with lines of stitching. Finally cut the material out from the interior and make the buttonhole stitching.

The several sections are joined together with small bars made with buttonhole stitching, except in such parts where the tiny loops are very near to each other and at those points the joining is made with two nearest loops, as may be seen in the photograph.

The lines of stitching which hold the design in proper shape should not be cut until the entire work has been finished.

MATERIAL: Organdie.
THREADS: Embroidery No. 80 in the bobbin and in the needle.
NEEDLE: No. 8.
TENSIONS: Both somewhat tight and even.

English Lace

MAKING THE BRAID

THIS lace is similar to that described in Lesson 13—"English Lace", except that the braid is not applied but made on the work. This gives more value to the work but, of course, increases the difficulty in its execution, as the braid must be reproduced exactly so as to obtain the desired effect.

Machine is to be prepared with Embroidery Thread No. 80 in the bobbin and Needle No. 8, which should be threaded with same class and number of thread. For the braid both tensions must be moderate and even; for the cording the upper tension moderate and the bobbin tension a little tight.

As a base use organdie on which the design should be reproduced as usual, then take a line of ordinary stitching around the outline.

Fill in all the space left for the braid with small stitches very close together so that they are compact, but not superimposed. Change the needle, inserting No. 19 and making the small lace points which resemble hemstitching. Draw a double thread from the machine and make these points, taking five stitches to unite the threads in between each of the points. At the same time take one stitch over the thread so as to form the outside border.

Then make the lace work in the background which is similar to that of English Lace and finish by cording all of the braid with a double strand of thread from the machine.

MATERIAL: Organdie.

THREADS: Embroidery No. 80 in the needle and in the bobbin.

NEEDLES: No. 8 for the braid.

No. 19 for the small lace points.

TENSIONS: For the braid and the small lace points both moderate and even; for the cording the upper tension moderate and the bobbin tension a little tight.

Zombori Lace

THIS is an artistic creation which consists of a neat and delicate lace point.

The machine should be prepared with Embroidery Thread No. 80 in the needle and in the bobbin. Needle No. 8. Tensions moderate and even for the braid and the lace points; for the cording and double stitching, the upper tension moderate and the bobbin tension a little tight.

After tracing the design on the organdie, which is used as a base, take a line of stitching over the outline and then make the braid which is the same as in "English Lace— Making the Braid" (Lesson No. 77), with the

only exception that a small space must be left on each side to make the small lace point, which has been explained in the above mentioned lesson. (See photograph).

After the braid has been finished, again insert Needle No. 8 to make the small lace points, beginning with the center of the figure. The center is made by taking stitches in two opposite diagonal lines forming small squares, then continue with the oval further down and make a point similar to Point "B" of Venetian Lace—First Stitches (Lessons 22 and 23). Then make the meshes on the sides of the figure.

Continue filling in the background with small bars of double stitching and finish by cording the outline for which purpose you will have to carry as a filler a strand of Irish Thread No. 60 with which the tiny loops shown in the photograph will be made. These loops are the same as those described in "Hedebo Embroidery" (Lesson No. 29).

MATERIAL: Organdie.

THREADS: Embroidery No. 80 in both parts. For the outline Irish Thread No. 60.

NEEDLES: No. 8. No. 19 for the fine lace points.

TENSIONS: For the braid and the lace points, both moderate and even; for the double stitch and the cording the upper tension moderate and the bobbin tension a little tight.

Irish Lace

THIS is a well known style of lace which, on account of its flexibility, is very suitable for the adornment of feminine garments. It requires a design with basic outlines which are repeated over the entire work.

The machine is to be prepared with Embroidery Thread No. 80 in the bobbin, and needle No. 7 which should be threaded with the same class of thread but No. 100. Both tensions are to be moderate and even for making flowers, the leaves and the trimmings in general. For the double stitch and the buttonhole stitch the upper tension moderate and the bobbin tension somewhat tight.

As a base use organdie on which the design is to be traced.

Around the outline carry as a guide a single strand of thread from the machine and apply it with reinforcing stitches, except for the flowers where a line of stitching must first be taken. The flowers are made, beginning with the small corded bars and then making the little eyelet which is made with buttonhole stitch. Continue with the petals, cutting out the material from the interior and then covering them with small stitches which start from the outer edge toward the center and vice-versa.

When finishing the first line of petals, which should be the nearest to the center, they should be cut out. They will then remain adhered to the central circle by their lower edge. Then fold upwards the upper part. Care should be taken that the stitches closely follow the outline.

Make under the first line of petals and almost at their base, a corded circle, to do which you will have to carry as a filler a double strand of thread from the machine. This circle serves to join the stitching with which the petals on the second row are made, and after completing they should be cut out in the same way as the previous petals. Then continue with the other layers.

Now begin to make the background; this consists of bars of double cording and small loops as will be seen in the photograph. Sections as indicated by "A" are made by cutting small pieces of material between both reinforcements and carrying on each side a double strand of thread from the machine so as to make the double cording.

For the grapes and the leaves take another set of hoops, insert organdie and trace the design. (See the enlarged reproduction in the inset). The grapes are made with a strand of Irish Thread No. 60 which is fastened half-way in the center of the grape, forming in this way two strands. These strands are crossed with each other, as you proceed, fastening at each crossing with a stitch and at the same time giving it a circular shape.

For the leaves make a line of stitching over the outline and then reinforce as usual. Afterward cut out the material from the interior and then fill in the space with stitching. Finish by making a buttonhole stitch on the outer edges, carrying as a filler a double strand of thread from the machine.

After the grapes and the leaves have been completed, they should be neatly cut out and applied on the places where they belong. The leaves are secured with a double cord which will form the vein which joins them and which must exactly fit with the stems already made (See "B"). The grapes are applied with one or more stitches taken in such a way that they may not be visible.

The lace is finished with a buttonhole stitch around both edges.

MATERIAL: Organdie.

THREADS: In the needle, Embroidery No. 100. In the bobbin, Embroidery No. 80. For the Grapes, Irish Thread No. 60.

NEEDLE: No. 7.

TENSIONS: For the flowers and ornamental work, both moderate and even. For the double stitch and buttonhole stitch, the upper tension moderate and the bobbin tension a little tight.

Lace With Gold Thread

THIS work is suitable for lace point trimmings on altar cloths, etc.

It is essential to be very careful in the preparation of the machine and to see that the tensions are correctly adjusted, varying them according to the particular section of the work.

To facilitate the making of this work, the lesson has been divided into two parts. The first part describes the embroidery with embroidery thread and the second part the work that is done with golden thread.

For the first part prepare the machine with embroidery thread No. 80 in the bobbin, needle No. 7 and embroidery thread No. 100 in the needle. Both tensions are to be moderate and even.

After the design has been traced on organdie which is used as a base, take a line of stitching over the outline and then reinforce with a single strand of thread from the machine. Then make the braid as per instructions contained in Lesson 60 ("Bone Lace Edging"), and make on the outside edges the small lace points which are identical with those described in Lesson 77.

For the second part prepare the machine with Gold Thread in the bobbin and in the needle. The needle must be of a suitable size. In the sample reproduced in the photograph needle No. 11 was used. The tensions should be somewhat loose and even.

Take a line of stitching over the center of the braid, as will be seen in the photograph. Make the lower lace points, which are made with stitches in two diagonal lines so as to form squares, then cross in pairs the lines of stitches of the upper lace points and leave, both at the beginning and at the end, two long strands of thread so as to tie them.

In crossing the center with a line of stitches take a stitch over the line previously made in order to form a spot after the lace has been completed.

The simplicity of the work requires the greatest perfection in the stitches so as to obtain the desired effect.

Insertion of Szepes Bone Lace

O N account of the severe lines of this work, it is essential to see that the different parts of it are made with great precision, as only in this way its artistic value, which is its main feature, will be fully appreciated.

The machine should be prepared by winding in the bobbin Embroidery Thread No. 80 and using No. 8 needle, which should be threaded with the same class and number of thread. For the cording, the upper tension must be moderate and the bobbin tension a little tight; for the balance of the work, both tensions are to be moderate and even.

After tracing the design on the organdie, which is used as a base, take a line of stitching around the outline. Then draw a single strand of thread from the machine and neatly reinforce, except in those parts where, as in "A", the stitching is taken over the interior line and corded on the exterior line at the same time that the small lace point is made, similar to that in Lesson No. 77.

Again insert needle No. 8 and make such parts as are covered with darning stitch in the same way as in Lesson No. 45 ("Bone Lace Insertions"). Begin with the smallest, that is, the small leaves and circles, then make the borders which are made with a variation of darning similar to that explained in Lesson No. 60 ("Bone Lace Edging").

With a double cord make the small bars in the background and finish by making the buttonhole stitch around the outlines. For this purpose baste a double strand of thread from the machine and carry another two strands as a filler.

MATERIAL: Organdie.

THREADS: Both in the needle and in the bobbin, No. 80 embroidery.

NEEDLES: No. 8 and No. 19 for the small lace point.

TENSIONS: For the cording, the upper tension moderate and the bobbin tension somewhat tight; for the balance of the work, both moderate and even.

A

Kis Koros Bone Lace Insertion

THIS insertion is another proof of the variety of combinations that may be made with many of the laces and embroideries already explained.

The machine should be prepared with embroidery thread No. 80 in the bobbin and needle No. 8 threaded with the same thread. For the lace points and darning, both tensions must be moderate and even, and for the double cord and the buttonhole stitch, the upper tension should be moderate and the bobbin tension somewhat tight.

After tracing the design on organdie, which is used as a base, take a line of stitching around the outline and carefully reinforce it with a single strand of thread from the machine. First make the sections that are covered with half stitch, in the same way as was described in Lesson 45—"Bone Lace Insertion". Continue with the darning, which is made by taking lines of stitches in a similar manner to that explained in connection with the small hemstitch in Lesson 62—"Venetian Lace", and then make over those lines of stitches any variations which may be desired.

The small hemstitching on the edges of the darning is then made, the threads being corded by bunches of two each in the spaces which were left empty for that purpose.

Then make a double cord for the little bars with loops which are seen in the background, and finish by taking a line of buttonhole stitching around the entire outline.

MATERIAL: Organdie.
THREADS: Embroidery thread No. 80 in the needle and the bobbin.
NEEDLE: No. 8.
TENSIONS: For the half stitch, lace points and darning, both moderate and even.
For the buttonhole stitch and the double cord, the upper tension moderate and the bobbin tension somewhat tight.

Rooniok Lace Edging

THE lace edging shown in the photograph requires absolute perfection in the stitching, in order that the work may not lose any of its merit, which principally consists in the simplicity of the design.

The machine is prepared with embroidery thread No. 80 in the bobbin and in the needle; needle No. 8. As a base use organdie. To make the braid, both tensions must be moderate and even. For the background the bobbin tension should be somewhat tight and the needle tension moderate.

After tracing the design in the usual way, take a line of stitching around the outline and neatly reinforce it with a single thread drawn from the machine. Then proceed to make the braid, following directions contained in Lesson 80—"Lace Points with Gold Thread", with the exception that instead of applying a gold thread in the center, a strand of highly mercerized twisted cotton is used. The small lace point on the edges is made as explained in Lesson 77.

Finally make the bars in the center with double stitch and small corded buttonholes.

MATERIAL: Organdie.

THREADS: Embroidery No. 80 both in the needle and the bobbin.

For the center of the braid, highly mercerized twisted cotton.

NEEDLE: No. 8.

TENSIONS: For the braid, both tensions moderate and even.

For the background, the upper tension moderate and the bobbin tension somewhat tight.

Cobweb Lace

THIS is a beautiful piece of work which gives the impression of having been made without the use of any material as a base. The greatest difficulty in making it lies in endeavoring to convey such an impression.

Use organdie on which the basic design is traced, in this case the vase, leaves and flowers. Prepare the machine with embroidery thread No. 80 in the bobbin, and needle No. 8 threaded with the same class and number of thread. The upper tension should be moderate and the bobbin tension somewhat tight.

Take a line of stitching around the entire

outline and drawing a single strand of thread from the machine reinforce carefully. Then make a hemstitching around the squares. To do so take three lines of stitches from one edge to the other and then reinforce the central line up to the point where the three lines are to be joined. Continue reinforcing up to the opposite edge but without reaching the edge, and finish the reinforcement of the line in the center. Repeat this operation until the entire square has been completed and finish it with two lines of stitching, as will be observed in the photograph. It is essential to maintain the same distance from one edge as the other.

Then make the network which forms the vase and the hemstitching which serves as ornamentation of vase. The style of this hemstitching is exactly the same as that used around the square.

The leaves are made by taking lines of stitching in the interior lengthwise and then making very small tapering bars in an opposite direction. The number and thickness of these bars may vary according to the size of the leaves.

The flowers are made in the same manner as the leaves, with the exception that the stitching in the interior is made crosswise to the petals. Some of the leaves have petals over them which are to be applied as per instructions in Lessons 43 and 44—"Artistic Embroidery on White Goods".

To make the background, change the threads in the machine, inserting embroidery thread No. 40 in the bobbin and enbroidery thread No. 60 in the needle and using needle No. 9. Both tensions are to be moderate and even.

First take lines of stitching from the edge to the parts already worked. These lines will form the base of the background. For this purpose, the background was previously divided into sections, as indicated in the photograph. Then over each one of these lines, make the lines of stitching which will form the circles, being careful to join the different sections in such a way that the union is not noticeable. To this end the threads of one section must exactly meet the threads of the next section, so as to convey the impression that there is but one continuous line of thread.

To conclude cord the outlines with a filler of Irish thread No. 60.

MATERIAL: Organdie.
THREADS: For the vase, leaves and flowers, embroidery No. 80 in the needle and in the bobbin.
For the background, embroidery No. 60 in the needle and No. 40 in the bobbin.
For the outlines, Irish thread No. 60.
NEEDLES: No. 8 for the vase, leaves and flowers.
No. 9 for the background.
TENSIONS: For cording in general, the upper tension moderate and the bobbin tension a little tight.
For the background, both moderate and even.

Macramé Prince Weave

THIS style of weave is one of the most popular of the handmade fringes and when made on the machine it is extremely easy to produce.

The machine is prepared with embroidery thread No. 80 in the needle and in the bobbin, and needle No. 8. Tensions are to be moderate and even.

As a base nainsook or other material of similar body is to be used. Cut the material out gradually as you apply the strands of Macramé Cord which form the background. These must be of suitable thickness. In the sample reproduced thread No. 14 was used. The strands are placed over the entire background, folded in two equal parts and secured

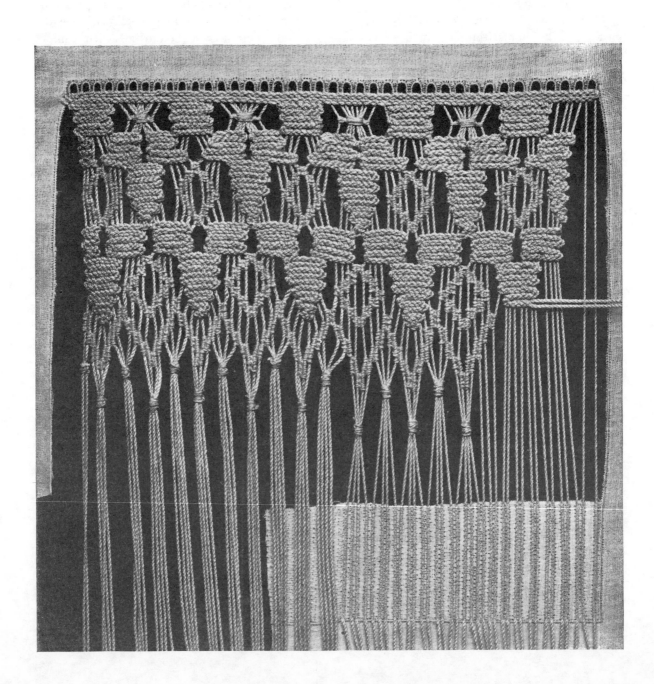

at the upper edge of the square at the point where they are divided into two. A slight reinforcement is made at the point of fastening, making a small loop. In this way from each strand of cord two strands are made (see photograph, upper part).

The two ends of each strand are now well stretched and secured with a slight reinforcement at the lower end of the square, taking care not to run the needle through these strands so that later on when the work has been finished they can be easily detached.

After making the weave in the background, change the threads and the tensions and insert in the bobbin Embroidery Thread No. 16. Place needle No. 11 and thread it with Macramé Thread No. 40, then tighten the tension of the bobbin.

Carry as many strands as the pattern calls for; in this case two strands, which should be of Thread No. 20. Intertwine them, fastening them at each crossing with a stitch that should take the thread of the lower weave.

The zig-zag as well as the knots shown in the photograph are made as explained in connection with darning in Lessons Nos. 6 and 7, "Hemstitch".

Finally cut out the material from the interior of the loops at the lower part and then pull the ends of the weaved threads so that these will become detached from the fabric and the work will be finished.

MATERIAL: Nainsook.

THREADS: To secure the weave, Embroidery No. 80 in the needle and in the bobbin.
For embroidery, Macramé Thread No. 40 in the needle and Embroidery Thread No. 16 in the bobbin. For the weave in the background, Macramé Thread No. 14.

NEEDLES: For Thread No. 80—Needle No. 8. For Macramé No. 40—Needle No. 11.

TENSIONS: For the work with embroidery thread, both moderate and even. For work with Macramé, the upper tension moderate and the bobbin tension a little tight.

Fancy Lace and Embroidery Points
SPECIAL

THE fancy points illustrated in the photo-graph differ entirely from those explained in previous lessons; the embroidered points because they are worked with raised stitching and the lace points because most of them are produced by cording, consequently their execution demands a higher grade of ability.

For the embroidered points prepare the machine with Embroidery Thread No. 60 in the bobbin, and needle No. 8 which should be threaded with Embroidery Thread No. 80. For the lace points the preparation is the same, except that the bobbin is also threaded with No. 80 thread. The tensions are to be adjusted according to the points to be made.

It is essential to follow in each case the instructions given in previous lessons on this important matter. As a rule, for the embroidered points the upper tension should be moderate and the bobbin tension a little tight, and for the lace points both are to be moderate and even.

The most suitable fabric is linen. In the sample shown, white linen was used but other colors can also be utilized, and by combining them with the appropriate shades of threads attractive effects are obtained.

The method to produce the embroidery and lace points shown in the photograph, which are only a few of the many that can be produced, is the following:

Point "A"—Cord six threads in one direction, covering the distance required, then cord another six threads at right angles. Continue cording threads, alternating in each direction always in groups of six, and taking care that all the angles are straight.

Point "B"—Cord eight threads in one direction, making the stitches diagonally. Repeat the same work with subsequent groups, always taking eight threads and being careful to take the stitches of each successive row in a direction contrary to that of the preceding.

Point "C"—First fill in space of the design with stitches so that the point to be produced will be raised, then take five stitches on top of each other which should end in the same place at both edges so as to form a group of threads; leave a space of from one-twelfth to one-eighth inch and do the same thing again and again until the entire space has been covered. Proceed in the same way, but in a contrary direction, in order that when the stitches pass over the previous ones they will form tiny squares. Then take lines of stitching in a diagonal direction in the following way: starting from the center of the first square take five stitches which, passing over the crossing of the previous threads, are fastened in the center of the next square and so an until the entire diagonal line has been completed, then making in the same way all the other lines that run in the same direction. Proceed in an identical manner with the opposite diagonal line.

Point "D"—Draw one thread and leave two threads in each direction, which should be reinforced so as to form a background of small squares. Cover one square with raised embroidery and in the following row cover three squares. In the next row cover five squares, then gradually diminish the number of squares covered in each subsequent row, keeping the same proportion. In this way a square will be produced in a diagonal direction to that of the threads of the material. Do as many squares as the space permits but taking care to leave the empty space indicated in the photograph.

Point "E"—Draw nine threads and leave four in one direction only, then cord each group of four. Separate the other threads in groups of six; begin half-way between the corded threads; take the two middle threads with two stitches, then one more thread on each side and then another on each side; this will give a total of six threads. Continue tying groups of six threads until completed.

Point "F"—Draw two threads and leave four in both directions, then reinforce. Run a line of stitches diagonally in one direction across every second row of squares, tying the angle of each square with two stitches. After crossing them in one direction, repeat the operation in an opposite diagonal direction.

Point "G"—Draw two threads and leave three in both directions, then reinforce. Run two strands of embroidery thread No. 20 in diagonal direction across each group of squares, tying the angle of each square with two stitches.

Point "H"—This point can be made in one or two rows, according to the width of the design. The lace point must be made between the two rows, taking in this case two threads at a time and fastening them with two or three stitches. Make the raised point over the entire space of the design, carrying at the same time two strands of Irish Thread of a suitable thickness and making at the crossings of the strands two or three stitches so as to form a knot.

Point "J"—This point is made by covering the space with stitches over which other stitches are taken in small groups, as was explained in Lessons Nos. 10 and 11—Point "B", "Fancy Stitches on White Goods", with the difference that in this case the outline must be followed and the entire space covered, except the veins of the leaves which must be made with the points known as "Turkish Point", dealt with in Lessons Nos. 19 and 20.

Point "K"—This is similar to point "A" but combined with "Turkish Point".

Point "L"—This is produced by following instructions in Lesson No. 50, "Imitation Velvet Embroidery", but with the exception that a finer needle is used and that the center is finished with "Turkish Point".

Point "M"—The space is filled in with stitches and over these make Point "D" of Lessons Nos. 10 and 11.

Point "N"—Draw two threads and leave four threads in each direction. Do not reinforce. Take one stitch at each corner of every square. This will give the square a rounded shape. At the next square take stitches forming a small spot and continue alternating these two points.

Finish by cording those parts of the design which are not raised and when getting to the foldings of the leaves do these in a manner similar to Point "H", but varying, if you wish, the cording applied.

The zig-zag may be made with one cord or with several, as the operator may choose.

MATERIAL: Linen.

THREADS: For the embroidered points— Embroidery No. 80 in the needle and Embroidery No. 60 in the bobbin.

For the lace points, Embroidery No. 80 both in the needle and in the bobbin.

For Point "H", Irish Thread.

NEEDLES: No. 8.

No. 19 for the Turkish Point.

TENSIONS: For the Embroidered Point, the upper tension moderate and the bobbin tension a little tight.

For the lace points, both moderate and even.

Fancy Embroidery For Dresses

TWO classes of embroidery, both of great usefulness, are described in this lesson. The first consists of leather applied on Mongol Crepe, the application of which may also be made on heavy fabrics. The second is made with wool applied on some suitable material. In this case the former, that is to say Mongol, Crepe, was used.

For the application of leather prepare the machine with Embroidery Thread No. 60 in the bobbin and sewing silk No. 00 in the needle. The silk must be of the same color as the leather. Needle No. 9. The bobbin tension must be a little tight and the upper tension moderate.

After inserting the material in the hoops, apply the leather over it and reproduce the design in the usual way. Take a line of very small stitches over the outline of the design and cut out the leather around the entire outline. Then cord with a double strand of thread from the machine, except in those sections where the embroidery is made with artificial silk. For that part take two strands of artificial silk and apply in the same direction, taking care that the stitches, securing the strands of silk, are at a distance of about ⅕ inch from each other. Finish by applying on the outline of each circle two strands of artificial silk, which are to be intertwined so that the stitches taken to secure one strand are covered by the other strand.

For the fancy work with wool, prepare the machine with wool of the necessary color

both in the needle and in the bobbin and use needle No. 18. The bobbin tension must be moderate and the upper tension a little tighter.

After the design has been traced, begin by covering it with long or short stitches, according to the requirements of the different sections. Take one stitch from "A" to "B", returning with a second stitch to "A", then a third stitch as far as "C", and repeat until finishing the entire section.

The veins are made in like manner, taking care that the length of stitch is suitable to the design.

MATERIALS: For the first, Mongol Crepe and Leather.
For the second, Mongol Crepe.

THREADS: For the first, in the needle, Sewing Silk No. 00 and in the bobbin Embroidery Thread No. 60.
For the second, thin wool, both in the needle and in the bobbin. For the interior and the outlines of the circles, Artificial Silk.

NEEDLES: For the silk, No. 9.
For the wool, No. 18.

TENSIONS: For the first, the upper tension moderate and the bobbin tension a little tight.
For the second, the upper tension a little tight and the bobbin tension moderate.

FIGURE 2

Embroidery With Mercerized Embroidery Cotton

THIS variety of embroidery is appropriate for attractive combinations in many pieces of ornamental work for the home.

The design must be of straight lines but it lends itself to any variation which the operator may wish to introduce.

The machine is prepared with mercerized thread No. 5 of a suitable color and needle No. 14, which is threaded with Embroidery Thread No. 20. The upper tension should be tight and the bobbin tension loose.

The material to be used is canvas, over which organdie should be placed as a reinforcement, and proceed in the same manner as has been explained in previous lessons; that is to say, count the meshes in accordance with the pattern which must be kept before you. The stitches should be long so as to cover the section that is being made from one end to the other and the colors are to be changed whenever necessary.

It must be borne in mind that the face of the work will appear on the side opposite to that on which you are working.

MATERIALS: Canvas.
           Organdie as a reinforcement.
THREADS: In the needle, Embroidery Thread No. 20.
         In the bobbin, Mercerized Embroidery Cotton No. 5.
NEEDLE: No. 14.
TENSIONS: The upper tension tight, the bobbin tension loose.

Embroidery With Metallic Cord

THIS embroidery is an appropriate ornamentation for coats-of-arms, crowns or
military insignias. It is generally made on
cloth, but silk, satin or linen may also be used.
The sample shown in the photograph was
made on cloth.

Prepare the machine with Embroidery
Thread No. 60 in the bobbin and needle No.
9, which should be threaded with gold sewing
silk No. 00. The upper tension must be moderate, the bobbin tension somewhat tight.

Trace the design, following instructions
contained in previous lessons, and take a line
of stitching around the outline. First fill in

with stitches those sections where the metallic cord is to be applied so as to give them raised effect, but taking care that this effect is more pronounced in the center line than at the edges.

Then take a strand of metallic cord and another strand of plain cord, which should be of the exact length required to cover the sections to be worked. Both threads are wound around the silk thread, separately by hand, which will serve to hold them, and are applied on the design diagonally, fastening each row with two stitches at the ends.

The stitches are to be taken in the lower part of the metallic cording and toward the center so that they may not be visible.

MATERIAL: Cloth.
Metallic Thread Corded and Plain.
THREADS: In the needle, Embroidery Sewing Silk No. 00 of gold color, in the bobbin, Embroidery No. 60.
NEEDLE: No. 9.
TENSIONS: The upper tension moderate and the bobbin tension somewhat tight.

Imitation Tapestry

ALTHOUGH it would seem that imitation of tapestry on a machine should be very complicated, as a matter of fact it is not so and all that is required is considerable neatness and care in placing the stitches, and of course, artistic taste in combining the different colors.

The machine should be prepared with Embroidery Thread No. 60 in the bobbin, needle No. 9, which should be threaded with Sewing Silk No. 00 of a suitable color. The upper tension must be moderate and the bobbin tension somewhat tight. As a base use canvas.

Keep before you the design to be reproduced and count the meshes according to the design, covering them with stitches in a diagonal direction. Repeat the stitches until the squares are well filled. In the work shown in the photograph six stitches were taken in each square.

When finishing leave the threads somewhat long so as to be able to tie them on the wrong side of the work.

MATERIAL: Canvas.

THREADS: Sewing Silk No. 00 in the needle and Embroidery No. 60 in the bobbin.

NEEDLE: No. 9.

TENSIONS: The upper tension moderate and the bobbin tension somewhat tight.

Embroidery on Leather

IN order that the operator may be able to produce this variety of embroidery, she must have mastered thoroughly Lessons 24 and 25 ("Shaded Embroidery"). Since in working on leather it is essential that the stitches be taken with the greatest accuracy and that the combination of the the shades also be above reproach. Other varieties of work can also be made with this kind of embroidery, such as Fancy Work, Raised Embroidery, etc.

The machine should be prepared with Embroidery Thread No. 60 in the bobbin and needle No. 9, threaded with sewing silk No. 00 of a suitable color. The upper tension

should be moderate and the bobbin tension a little tight.

The material may be chamois, kid, etc. Place organdie on the wrong side. The material used in the sample shown in the photograph was kid leather. After inserting the material into the hoops, trace the design according to instructions contained in previous lessons and take a line of stitching over the outline, then reinforce this line of stitching with a strand of thread from the machine. In this manner a slightly raised effect will be obtained and this, in addition to its attractive appearance, will also serve to prevent the leather from splitting when it is being em-

broidered. After finishing the shaded embroidery, press the work with an iron as was explained in Lessons 24 and 25, thus concluding a piece of work of real merit and beauty.

The method to be followed in making the dog's head shown in the other photograph is simple. This novelty is a creation of the Singer Embroidery Academy of Santiago, Chile, South America.

Use embroidery thread No. 60 in the bobbin and needle No. 9, threaded with sewing silk No. 00 of an appropriate color. The bobbin tension to be moderate and the needle tension somewhat tight.

Apply strands of wool of a suitable color in the proper place and secure them with a line of stitching over the center of the strand in a lengthwise direction, then thread the needle with silk of the required color and make the tongue and the eye. Then take a carding brush and following the direction of the strands that have been applied, card the wool carefully so to properly stretch it.

MATERIALS: Kid leather and organdie as a reinforcement.
For work with wool—wool in balls and skeins.

THREADS: In the needle, Sewing Silk No.00. In the bobbin, Embroidery Thread No. 60.

NEEDLE: No. 9.

TENSIONS: For the shaded embroidery, the upper tension moderate and the bobbin tension a little tight.
For embroidery with wool, the upper tension a little tight and the bobbin tension moderate.

Bengal Lace

IN the production of this simple and beautiful variety of lace, loud colors, appropriate to the country of origin of this work, are to be selected.

The machine should be prepared with embroidery No. 60 in the bobbin, and needle No. 9, threaded with sewing silk No. 00 of a violet color. Both tensions must be moderate and even.

As a reinforcement use organdie on which the design is to be traced as usual, then around the outline take a line of stitching and neatly reinforce it, drawing from the machine a single strand of thread. Change the threads,

inserting both in the bobbin and in the needle sewing silk No. 00 of a color to match and begin the darning, which is similar to that explained in Lesson 31, "Battenberg Embroidery".

After finishing the darning, again change the threads and insert embroidery thread No. 60 in the bobbin and violet sewing silk No. 00 in the needle. Then make the filling in all parts that are worked with a raised embroidery stitch, using cotton of the same color as the silk and following the method outlined in Lesson No. 8, "Scalloping and Raised Embroidery—Satin Stitch". Now adjust the tension a little tighter and make the raised embroidery stitch. Then make the bars which are similar to those described in Lesson No. 5, "Richelieu Embroidery", with the exception that two lines of stitching must be taken before cording and that silk of a suitable color must be used both in the needle and in the bobbin.

After finishing one bar, cord the next until reaching the place where they join, then stop cording temporarily and take a line of stitching to the first bar, then to the one you are making. Then with a second line of stitching return to the starting point and from that point cord up to the point where the cording was stopped. To do this draw a double strand of thread from the machine. Cut the strand of thread and continue cording to the first bar.

Finish by applying on the edges of the raised embroidery, four strands of golden thread. In applying this thread the stitches must be a little distant from each other.

MATERIAL: Organdie.
THREADS: For the stitching and the raised embroidery, in the needle sewing silk No. 00, in the bobbin embroidery thread No. 60.
For the balance of the work, sewing silk No. 00 both in the needle and in the bobbin.
For the edges, Gold Thread.
For the filling, colored cotton.
NEEDLE: No. 9.
TENSIONS: For the raised embroidery, the upper tension moderate and the bobbin tension a little tight.
For the stitching and the darning, both moderate and even.

Crochet Points

THE crochet point lace shown in the photograph is suitable for all kinds of white goods. The edges may be either curved or straight, as may be desired.

The machine should be prepared with Embroidery Thread No. 30 in the bobbin and needle No. 11 threaded with Embroidery Thread No. 40. Both tensions are to be moderate and even, except for the parts that are corded, where the bobbin tension should be somewhat tight.

As a base use organdie on which the design is to be traced, than take a line of stitching around the outline and reinforce with a single

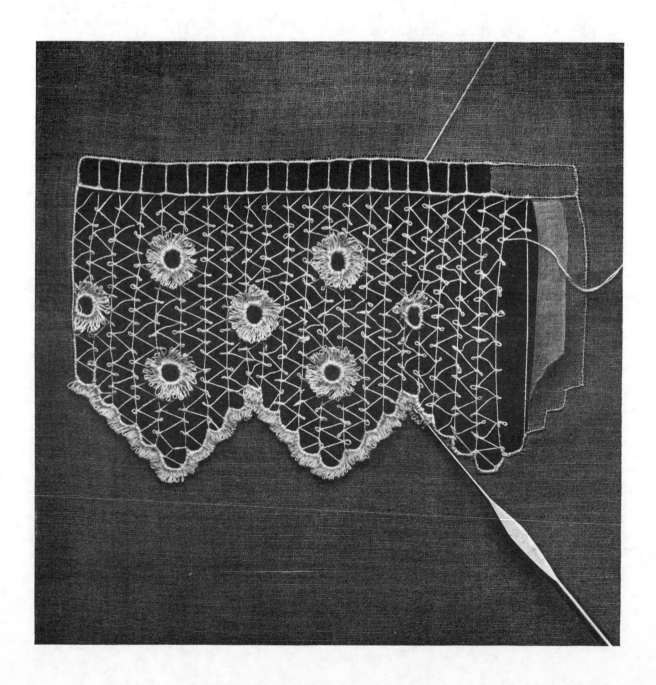

strand of thread from the machine, which will be used as a filler.

Run lines of stitching from one edge to the other. These lines must be at a distance of one-fifth of an inch from each other. Then, starting from the upper edge, take a line of stitching in a diagonal direction until reaching the next edge, fasten it with one stitch, return in a diagonal direction until getting to the first line of stitching where it should be fastened in the same manner.

Then make a little loop, using a crochet needle. A similar loop is to be made at the end of each diagonal line of stitching as may be seen in the photograph.

For the little flowers begin by making the eyelet in the center. This is made by carrying a strand of thread which should be corded. On the edge make loose loops, giving them the proper shape with the aid of a crochet needle. This needle should be raised from the work a little. Take one stitch in the buttonhole and another one to link the thread of the crochet needle and continue in the same way making loose loops close together until the eyelet has been completely made.

It is advisable to take as a model the loop that was made in the first place so that all the others are the same. The lower edge of the lace points is to be made precisely in the same manner.

Finally cord the small bars of the upper edge and then with a strand of darning thread do the same with the edges and sides.

MATERIAL: Organdie.

THREADS: In the needle, Embroidery No. 40. In the bobbin, Embroidery No. 30. For the cording, darning cotton.

NEEDLE: No. 11.

TENSIONS: Both moderate and even, except for the cording, where the bobbin tension should be a little tight.

Medallions

THIS is a difficult piece of embroidery particularly because of its small size. It requires considerable accuracy and neatness in order to be able to follow the lines of the design and so produce satisfactory results.

The machine is prepared with Laucil Silk both in the needle and in the bobbin; needle No. 7. Both tensions should be moderate and even.

Trace the design on bolting cloth of very close weave or a fine linen; take a line of stitching over the outline, being careful that it does not lose its shape, and begin by filling the space of the figure with "Granite Stitch", as

explained in Lesson 72. Then continue with the circle, which will serve as a frame and is made with a sort of raised stitch, but without any filling.

The small border is made with lines of stitching which should follow the design. After doing all the parts in black, change the silk and insert embroidery thread No. 80 in the bobbin and needle No. 8 which should be threaded with sewing silk No. 00 of a suitable color, and tighten the bobbin tension somewhat.

The small flowers are made with raised stitches on the bias, which will give them a very attractive appearance.

Then cut out the material from the outside of the border, which takes the place of a frame and leave sufficient material to permit the reinforcing of it on the back as is the custom with this kind of work.

The above instructions refer to Figure No. 1, the background of which has not been done. The background may be made in different ways, as for example—that shown in Figure No. 3 which was made in its entirety with "Granite Stitch" (Lesson 72). It is different from Figure No. 2, which is a combination of "Granite Stitch" and "Silk Stitch" (Lessons 24 and 25).

The flower pot was made with "Granite Stitch" and the flowers with "Silk Stitch", but both the pot and the flowers can be made with "Silk Stitch" if so desired.

MATERIAL: Bolting Cloth—of a very close weave.

THREADS: For the colored parts, in the needle Sewing Silk No. 00 and in the bobbin Embroidery Thread No. 80.
For the figure and the frame border, Laucil Silk in the bobbin and in the needle.

NEEDLES: For the Laucil Silk No. 7.
For the colored parts, No. 8.

TENSIONS: For the work with Laucil Silk, both moderate and even.
For the parts in color, the upper tension moderate and the bobbin tension a little tight.

Mirecourt Bone Lace Edging

THIS lace edging is one more proof of the beautiful combinations that can be produced with Bone Lace.

The machine is to be prepared with Embroidery Thread No 80 in the bobbin, and needle No. 7, which should be threaded with Embroidery Thread No. 100. The tensions are to be moderate and even for the "Half Stitch" and for the "Diamond Stitch", whereas for the double stitch and the buttonhole stitch the bobbin tension should be somewhat tighter.

As a base use organdie on which the design is to be traced in the usual way and afterward

a line of stitching must be taken around the outline, carrying as a filler a single thread from the machine.

The material is gradually cut out as you progress with the work in the parts where the "Half Stitch" is made (see "A"—"B" in the photograph), making at the same time the small bars ("C"), which are formed by cording the threads in groups of two at the center, and leaving small uncorded spaces at the ends. Then make the sections that require darning stitch.

For the small lace points as per letter "D", cut out the material and run lines of stitching as in "E" to "F" then do the same from "G" to "H", thus forming squares of about one-fifth of an inch. Then take a line of stitching through the center of these squares and re-inforce it with a second line of stitching as will be seen in the photograph. Afterward take a line of stitching running in a zig-zag on each side of the central line of stitches already taken. These zig-zag lines should be reinforced in the same manner as was done with the central line.

The same work should be made crosswise with the exception that when reinforcing the last of the three lines of stitching, a circle of darning should be made.

The lace work is finished by cording the lines of stitching that form the first squares; that is to say, those close to the lower edge and making at the same time, at each crossing of the threads, the small corded bars which join the squares.

Similar lace points are to be made in such places as the design calls for. Then make the small bars which join the sections made with darning stitch with those made with "Half Stitch".

To finish the lower part cut out the material, leaving a small border ("J") and form each loop with two lines of stitching. The second will serve as a reinforcement of the first.

Then take two lines of stitching to form the semi-circles which cross the loops and carrying as a filler two double strands of thread from the machine, make the double stitch and do a tiny loop at the end of the larger loop.

The lace work leaves that are superimposed should be made in accordance with instructions contained in Lesson 60, "Bone Lace Edging", and then applied on the work.

Finally make the outline with a buttonhole stitch, bearing in mind that on the upper edge this stitch must be made toward the material, both in applying the lace-edging and when the lace has been made directly on the material.

MATERIAL: Organdie.

THREADS: Embroidery No. 100 in the needle.
Embroidery No. 80 in the bobbin.

NEEDLE: No. 7.

TENSIONS: For the "Half Stitch" and "Darning Stitch", both moderate and even.
For the "Double Stitch" and "Buttonhole Stitch", the upper tension moderate and the bobbin tension a little tight.

Fancy Work of Raffia Straw

THIS is a new variety of work, of practical usefulness and great beauty. It is suitable for handbags, girls hats and fancy articles in general. It was created by the Singer organization in Berlin, Germany.

The machine is to be prepared with Embroidery thread No. 60 in the bobbin and needle No. 9, threaded with sewing silk No. 00 of the same color as the Raffia Straw used. Both tensions should be moderate and even.

As a base use cambric or some other similar material and trace the design on it in the usual way.

Select strips of Raffia Straw of the width

and color desired. Fold the borders under and apply on the fabric, in separate sections, as shown in the photograph.

First make the background, bearing in mind that the strips of straw are fastened at their ends with a line of stitching and in accordance with the design. After the green Raffia has been applied, proceed in the same way with the other colors and then apply the strips which divide the squares. These should be fastened with stitches about one-fifth of an inch apart, and a similar procedure will be followed with the five strips which run parallel with the length of the design.

As may be understood from the above, while this work is simple, it requires considerable care in order to obtain a beautiful effect, such as shown in the photograph.

MATERIALS: Raffia Straw.
              Cambric.
THREADS: In the needle, Sewing Silk No. 00.
              In the bobbin, Embroidery No. 60.
NEEDLE: No. 9.
TENSIONS: Both moderate and even.

Imitation Embossed Velvet

EMBOSSED velvet is used in ornamental work for the church, also in general upholstery work. It is very suitable in making flowers and figures.

The machine should be prepared with embroidery thread No. 60 in the bobbin and sewing silk No. 00 of an appropriate color in the needle. The size of the needle must be in accordance with the thickness of the material. In the sample shown in the photograph twenty layers of superimposed material were used and needle No. 11. The bobbin tension should be somewhat tight and the needle tension rather loose. As a base use satin and

apply organdie on the wrong side. Place on the satin as many layers of scrim and interlining as the desired thickness of the velvet may require and on top of these layers of material, place organdie on which the design shall have been previously traced, then baste together all the different materials.

On account of the thickness of the work, a set of hoops cannot be used. This however, is no disadvantage inasmuch as, due to the nature of the work, the hoops can very well be dispensed with.

The embroidery part consists in taking lines of stitches with suitable colors as closely as possible so that in the end they will form a compact surface. Then apply on the organdie that is placed on the wrong side of the satin a solution of mucilage. When the mucilage is dry you may proceed to remove the upper materials. To do this use a very sharp knife and scrape with great care the lines of stitching over the organdie. This is the only difficult part of the work, inasmuch as the lower layers become easily detached once the lines of stitching have been cut and may be taken out one by one until the satin is uncovered. Very carefully remove the lint.

The silk threads that were used in stitching over the surface of the design, after the several layers of material have been removed, will give an effect of embossed velvet, provided that all the stitching has been made very compact. The general appearance of the work will be very attractive.

MATERIALS: Satin as a base.
Organdie, scrim and interlining.

THREADS: In the needle, Sewing Silk No. 00. In the bobbin, Embroidery Thread No. 60.

NEEDLE: No. 11.

TENSIONS: The bobbin tension a little tight and needle tension rather loose.

Sculpture Reproduction

THE amphora reproduced in the photograph is a further proof of the perfection that can be attained in embroidery work.

The machine should be prepared with embroidery thread No. 60 in the bobbin, needle No. 8, threaded with embroidery thread No. 80. Both tensions to be moderate and even.

As a base use some elastic material, such as Jersey or some other similar fabric, as it is necessary that the material should yield in order that the work may show a raised effect.

For the background use satin, black velvet or some other similar dark fabric, as in this way the work will neatly stand out.

After the design has been traced, begin to cover completely with silk stitches similar to those explained in Lessons 24 and 25, "Shaded Embroidery". After this has been finished, change the tensions, making them somewhat tight and even. Make the small raised ornamental work and then you will be ready to apply the work on the background selected. Secure the figure with lines of stitching and fill it with cotton, so as to give it the required embossing; and continue fastening the balance of the edge. If a thin or small handle is required make it directly upon the background of the work, otherwise follow same method as described for the amphora.

MATERIALS: For the amphora, Jersey.
For the background, satin or velvet.

THREADS: In the needle, Embroidery Thread No. 80.
In the bobbin, Embroidery Thread No. 60.

NEEDLE: No. 8.

TENSIONS: For the silk stitching, both moderate and even.
For the balance of the work, both somewhat tight and even.

Embroidery on Wood

THE wood on which the work is made must be at the most $1/25$ of an inch thick. Oak, Cedar, Mahogany, etc., may be used and it must be polished on both sides in order that it may have the necessary smoothness and flexibility to permit the threads to go through without breaking and also so that the wood itself may not split when it is worked.

The sample shown in the photograph was made on oak veneer with two reinforcements of organdie applied on the wrong side of the wood, in opposite directions.

The machine should be prepared with embroidery thread No. 60 in the bobbin, and needle No. 9 threaded with sewing silk No. 00 of an appropriate color. The tensions to be moderate and even.

After tracing the design in the usual way, take a line of stitching around the outline, then proceed to make the details such as the nose, the mouth and the ears, keeping before you the model so as to obtain the greatest accuracy, and continue by making the rest of the head until completing it, following instructions in Lessons 24 and 25, "Shaded Embroidery".

Embroidery on wood can also be made by combining Shaded Embroidery (Lessons 24 and 25) with Artistic Shaded Embroidery, Lesson 71.

MATERIALS: Oak Veneer.
As a reinforcement, organdie.

THREADS: In the needle, Sewing Silk No. 00. In the bobbin, Embroidery Thread No. 60.

NEEDLE: No. 9.

TENSIONS: Both moderate and even.

Smyrna Rug

THE photograph reproduces in full size a section of a Smyrna Rug which will convey an idea of the quality of this work. The materials best adapted as a base are those having an open weave and at the same time sufficient strength, such as canvas or other similar fabrics. In the sample reproduced canvas was used.

The method to be followed and the way to prepare the machine are identical with those explained in Lesson 21 (Smyrna Embroidery) but as this kind of work is much larger and heavier, it is not necessary to use the hoops.

First embroider the basic features of the design in order that the colors are not mixed and to preserve neatness in the individual outline of these features. Then do the background. Afterward cut out all the strands of the wool, beginning with the basic features of the design and finishing with the gackbround.

MATERIAL: Canvas.

THREADS: In the needle, Sewing Silk, No. 00. In the bobbin, Embroidery Thread No. 40.

NEEDLE: No. 9.

TENSIONS: Both somewhat tight and even.

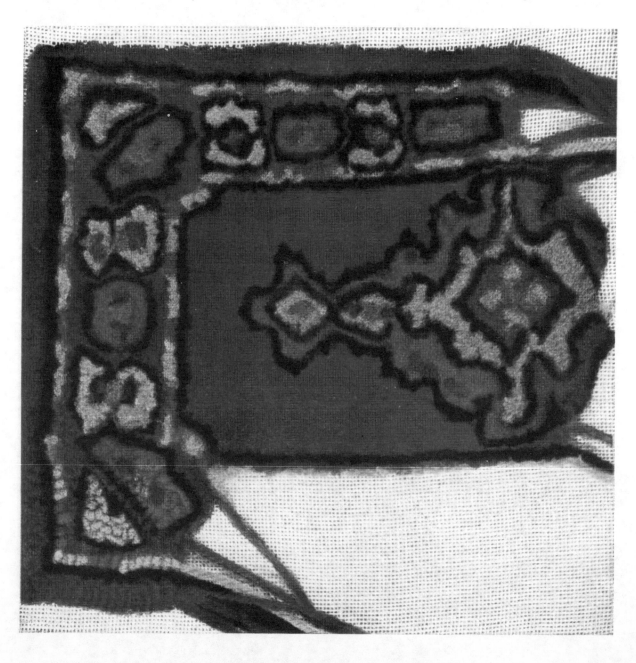

SINGER

INSTRUCTIONS

FOR

ART EMBROIDERY

AND

LACE WORK

FIFTH COURSE

OF

STUDY

▼▼

SINGER SEWING MACHINE COMPANY

Combination

THE combination illustrated in the photo-graph was made with Mongol Crepe. Several embroidery points were used, namely, "Scalloping and Raised Embroidery--Satin Stitch", (Lesson 78) "Turkish Point" as explained in "Needle Point Lace and Venetian Richelieu Lace", (Lessons 19 and 20), "Blond Lace" (Lesson 33) and "Artistic Lace Points" as per Lessons 39 and 40.

Bed Spread

THIS elaborate bed spread was made with closely woven linen.

The following varieties of embroideries and lace were used: "English or Eyelet Embroidery (Lesson 3,) "Richelieu Embroidery" (Lesson 5), "Scalloping and Raised Embroid-ery—Satin Stitch" (Lesson 8), "Fancy Stitches" on White Goods", (Lessons 10 and 11), "Filet Lace" (Lesson 15), "Artistic Embroidery on White Goods" (Lessons 39 and 40), "Bone Lace Insertions" (Lesson 45) and "Venetian Lace", (Lesson 62).

In the photograph shown on this page, which is an enlargement of a section of the same bed spread, an idea will be gained of the perfection of its execution.

Bed Sheet

THIS piece of work is further proof of the variety of embroidery stitches that can be utilized in machine embroidery. It was made on linen and is a combination of the following styles of embroidery:

"Hemstitching", (Lessons 6 and 7), "Scalloping and Raised Embroidery—Satin Stitch", (Lesson 8), "Letters and Monograms", (Lesson 9), "Mexican Drawn Work", (Lessons 27 and 28), "Hedebo Embroidery" (Lesson 29), "Battenberg Embroidery", (Lesson 31), "Spanish Point Lace", (Lessons 55 and 56) and "Genoese Net" (Lessons 57 and 58).

Table Cover

THIS attractive table runner was made on linen. The following varieties of embroidery work were combined:

"English Embroidery", (Lesson 3), Scalloping and Raised Embroidery—Satin Stitch", (Lesson 8), "Filet Lace", (Lesson 15), "Needle Point Lace and Venetian Richelieu Lace", (Lessons 19 and 20), "Artistic Embroidery on White Goods", (Lessons 39 and 40), and "Malta Lace", (Lesson 59).

Boudoir Doll Lamp

THIS excellent piece of work, consisting of a Boudoir Doll Lamp, was made by following instructions in connection with "Applique on Net", (Lesson 12), "Brussels Lace", (Lesson 14) and "Embroidery on Net", (Lesson 18).

White Lace Cushion

THIS attractive original piece of work was made on net and cotton crepe and then applied on a silk satin cushion.

The following styles of embroidery were used:

"Hemstitching", (Lessons 6 and 7), "Embroidery on Net", (Lesson 18), "English Point Lace", (Lessons 37 and 38), and "Artistic Embroidery on White Goods" (Lessons 43 and 44).

Altar Cloth

THE delicate piece of embroidery work shown in the photograph was made on linen net and proves the degree of beauty and accuracy of execution that can be attained with the "Fancy Lace"as per Lesson 36, which is the only kind of embroidery work used in this Altar Cloth.

The other circumstance which enhances the merit of this work is the fact that it was perfectly executed by a pupil who has only one arm. This pupil studied embroidery at the Higher Singer Embroidery School in Buenos Aires. It is a clear demonstration of what can be accomplished with perservance and application and deserves special mention.

Table Runner

THIS runner was made on linen and contains the following varieties of embroidery: "Scalloping and Raised Embroidery—Satin Stitch", (Lesson 8), "Needle Point Lace and Venetian Richelieu Lace", (Lessons 19 and 20), "Bone Lace Insertions",(Lesson 45) and "Bone Lace Edging" (Lesson 60).

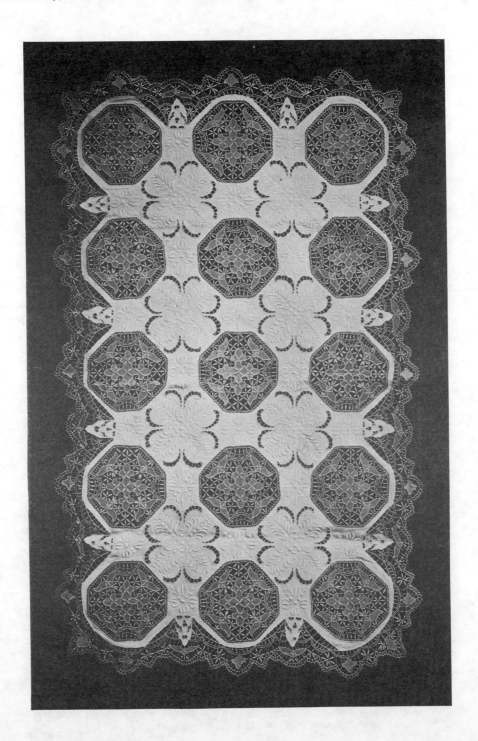

Kimono

THIS BEAUTIFUL KIMONO MADE ON COTTON CREPE WAS EMBROIDERED WITH
"SHADED EMBROIDERY" (LESSONS 24 AND 25)

Towel

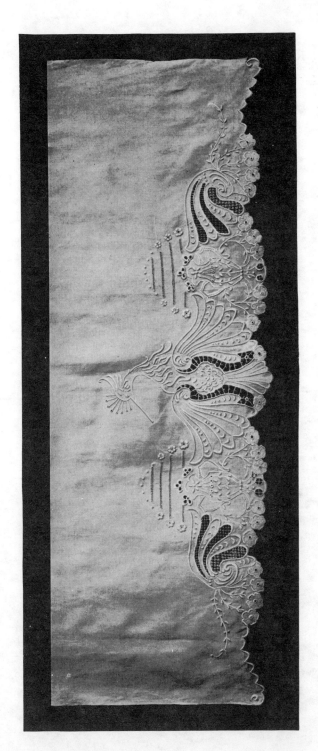

THE towel shown in the photograph proves the value of simple embroidery points when they are correctly made and artistically combined.

Closely woven linen was used and the following embroidery points were used: "English or Eyelet Embroidery", (Lesson 3), "Hemstitching" (Lessons 6 and 7), "Scalloping and Raised Embroidery—Satin Stitch", (Lesson 8), "Fancy Stitches on White Goods", (Lessons 10 and 11), "Needle Point Lace and Venetian Richelieu Lace" (Lessons 19 and 20), and finally "Fancy Lace Points" similar to those explained in Lessons 41 and 42 ("Renaissance Lace").

Tea Cozy

THIS nice looking piece of work has been made on organdie with "English Embroidery" (Lesson 3), "Richelieu Embroidery", (Lesson 5), "Scalloping and Raised Embroidery —Satin Stitch" (Lesson 8), "Turkish Point" as explained in "Needle Point Lace and Venetian Richelieu Lace", (Lessons 19 and 20) and "Teneriffe Wheels" (Lesson 26).

The lace edging was made with "English Lace—Applying the Braid", (Lesson 13).

Tray Cloth

THIS tray cloth was made on linen with "Scalloping and Raised Embroidery—Satin Stitch", (Lesson 8), "Turkish Point" as explained in "Needle Point Lace and Venetian Richelieu Lace", (Lessons 19 and 20), Venetian Lace—First Stitches", (Lessons 22 and 23), "Venetian Lace—Faces and Figures", (Lessons 63 and 64), and "Raised Embroidery on Net" (Lesson 66).

The attractive lace edging was made with "Crochet Lace" (Lesson 51).

Fancy Box

THIS was made on purple satin, orna- were made with beads as explained in
mented with fancy braid. The flowers "Bead Work" (Lesson 47).

Window Panel

THE work shown in the photograph was made on linen and contains the following varieties of embroidery: "English Embroidery" (Lesson 3), "First Openwork Stitches" (Lesson 4), "Richelieu Embroidery" (Lesson 5), "Scalloping and Raised Embroidery—Satin Stitch" (Lesson 8), "Fancy Stitches on White Goods" (Lessons 10 and 11), "Filet Lace" (Lesson 15), "Bone Lace—First Applique" (Lesson 17), and "Needle Point Lace and Venetian Richelieu Lace" (Lessons 19 and 20).

Runner For Dresser

IN order that you may fully appreciate the degree of perfection attained in the production of this piece of work, we have reproduced half of it only so as to permit the different points to be seen in detail. We recommend a close study of the photograph, if possible with a magnifying glass, and you will see that it will be hard to improve upon the finish of this work.

It was made on linen with "Scalloping and Raised Embroidery—Satin Stitch" (Lesson 8), "Filet Lace", (Lesson 15), "Fancy Lace Work on White Goods", (Lessons 39 and 40,) "Malta Lace", (Lesson 59) and Venetian Lace" (Lesson 62).

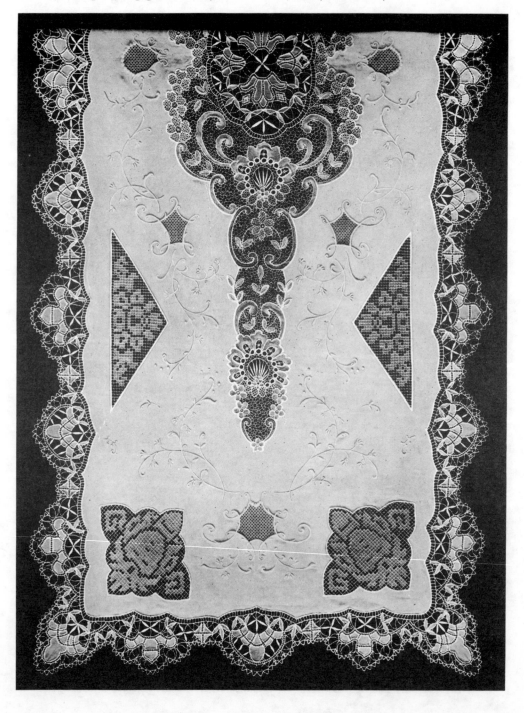

Lamp Shade

THIS shade was made on organdie, using styles of embroidery described in the First Course. The different styles of enbroidery were combined in such an artistic way that the effect is very attractive. The following varieties of embroidery were used: "English Embroidery", (Lesson 3), "Scalloping and Raised Embroidery—Satin Stitch", (Lesson 8), "Fancy Stitches on White Goods" (Lessons 10 and 11), "Filet Lace" (Lesson 15), "Bone Lace—First Applique" (Lesson 17), "Needle Point Lace and Venetian Richelieu Lace", (Lessons 19 and 20), and Venetian Lace—First Stitches", (Lessons 22 and 23).

Handkerchief Case

THE handkerchief case shown in the photograph was made on organdie with "Rococo Embroidery", (Lesson 48), letters "C" and "E" were made following instructions given in Lessons 67 and 68 in connection with "Embroidery with Gold or Silver Thread and Persian Embroidery".

Picture

THE picture reproduced shows that it is possible to produce on a sewing machine real works of art. This picture was made at the Singer Studios in the City of New York. It was entirely made with "Granite (Round) Stitch", (Lesson 72).

Curtains

THE curtains reproduced have been made on linen with the following varieties of embroidery stitches: "English or Eyelet Embroidery" (Lesson 3), "First Openwork Stitches", (Lesson 4) "Richelieu Embroidery", (CutWork),(Lesson 5),"Scalloping and Raised Embroidery—Satin Stitch", (Lesson 8), "Bone Lace—First Applique", (Lesson 17) and "Needle Point Lace and Venetian Richelieu Lace" (Lessons 19 and 20).

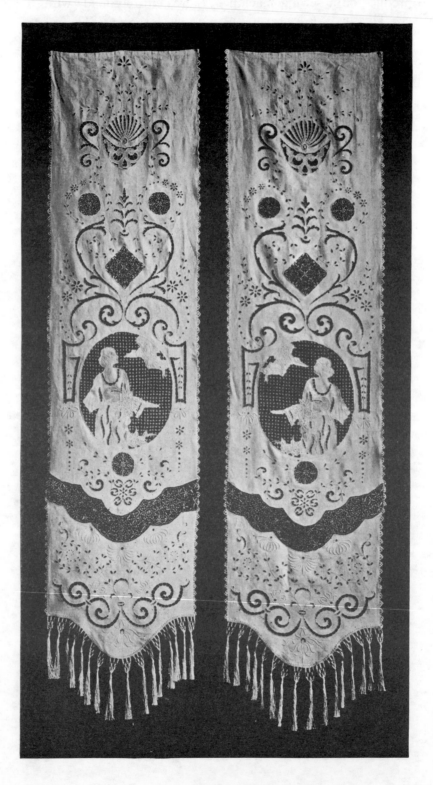

Parasol

THE model reproduced in the photograph was made on organdie with "Duchess Lace", (Lessons 52 and 53), and "Venetian Lace" (Lesson 62).

The different sections were sewn together and applied on gauze and the finish was made with cording as explained in Lesson 2 ("Cording"). The frame was lined with cream color cotton crepe.

Sofa Cushion

EMBROIDERED IN COLORS

THIS cushion, which is a piece of work of great beauty, was made with "Shaded Embroidery" (Lessons 24 and 25), and, as may be noticed in the photograph, a fabric made of golden net thread was used as a base. The balance of the cushion was covered with green taffeta.

Slippers and Bag

THE attractive and beautiful articles shown in the photograph are further examples of the variety that can be produced in raffia straw work (Lesson 96). They were made at the Singer Studios in Berlin, Germany.

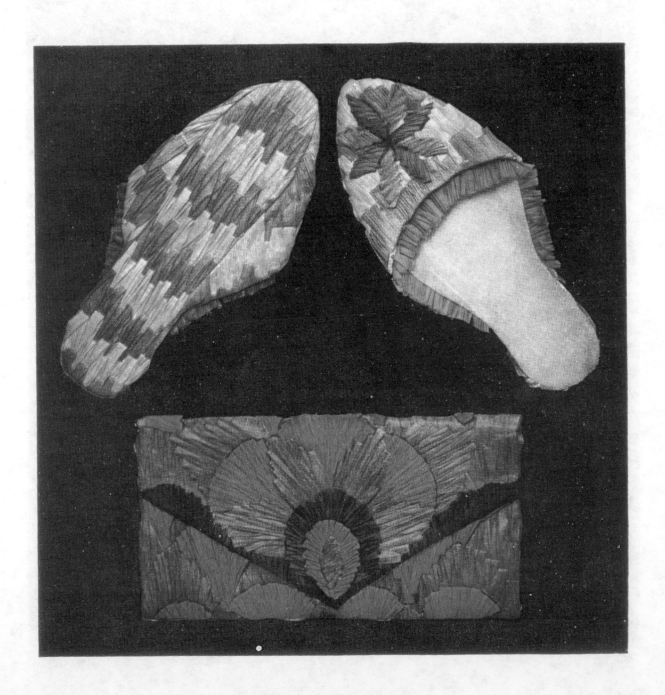

Baby Dress and Cap

CLUNY LACE, (Lesson 35) is particularly suitable for this variety of work. The entire dress and cap were made with this style of embroidery only.

Imitation Pen and Ink Drawing

THIS is a class of work where the operator must show, not only complete mastery of embroidery, but also her own individual artistic taste, since the reproduction of the models must be accurate and life-like so as to obtain the desired effect, especially when reproducing portraits. This work is usually made on organdie or bolting cloth.

The machine should be prepared with embroidery thread No. 60 in the bobbin and needle No. 7, threaded with Laucil Silk. The upper tension should be moderate and the bobbin tension a little tight.

After tracing the design, a line of running stitches should be taken around the outline, being particularly careful to neatly show the profile. Begin with the hair, which should be made with long stitches following its natural undulation, then make the features on the face until the entire face has been completed, and finish with the reproduction of the clothing. The profile and the isolated lines must be made with stitches on the bias.

Amphora

THE work reproduced on this page is conclusive proof of the perfection attained in the technique of machine embroidery and also proves that it is feasible to combine delicate workmanship with severe lines of an imposing effect.

This amphora was embroidered at the Singer Studios of London, England, by following instructions contained in Lesson 98, "Reproduction of Sculpture."

Recapitulation of Points

DARNING HEMSTITCHING POINT—This point is mentioned in Lesson No. 4 and in Lessons Nos. 6 and 7. It is made upon lines of running stitches and in an opposite direction to the running stitches, taking one stitch between each of the above mentioned lines until one row has been completed. Give half a turn to the hoops and make the second row, continuing in the same manner until the entire space has been darned. These stitches must be very close together so as to obtain a very compact weave.

BUTTONHOLE STITCH—This was mentioned for the first time in Lessons Nos. 6 and 7.

A strand of darning cotton is basted and a double strand of thread drawn from the machine is carried as a filler, securing it with one stitch. This filler is placed on the inner part, that is to say, that part which goes over the lace stitch; one stitch is taken on the edge of the fabric, another between the fabric and the threads and the third on the right hand side of the fabric, being careful that the stitches are as close as possible.

DARNING FILET STITCH—This was mentioned for the first time in Lesson No. 15.

Take lines of running stitches in the direction of the mesh and secure the ends of each line of stitches with two stitches, then make the lines running in an opposite direction, thus forming small squares. The Filet Darning Stitch differs from the Darning Hemstitch Point in that it is more transparent, because it contains a smaller number of stitches.

DOUBLE STITCH—Mentioned for the first time in Lesson No. 17.

Take a line of running stitches from one edge to the other, and draw from the machine a double strand of thread which will serve as a filler. Take three stitches, the first on the left of the line of stitching, the second on the right, that is to say, between the stitching and the thread, and the third on the right of the thread. The threads must be of equal thickness in order that both edges shall be even. Bear in mind that the size of the small bars must be in proportion with the class of material. If thicker bars are desired increase the number of lines of running stitches and of the strands to be used as filling. This is the difference between the double stitch and the buttonhole stitch.

NEEDLE POINT LACE—See Lessons Nos. 19 and 20.

TURKISH POINT—Was mentioned for the first time in Lessons Nos. 19 and 20.

The needle and the threads must be suitable to the fabric to be used. Carry a single strand of thread from the machine as a filler and take five stitches on both sides of the filler in a zig-zag.

VENETIAN HALF STITCH—This was mentioned for the first time in Lessons Nos. 22 and 23.

After cutting out a little piece from the interior of the fabric, beginning with the widest part, draw a strand of thread which must be carried as a filling and between the thread and the edge of the material adjust the distance as the stitch will call for. Cord the thread with two stitches taken in the space of $\frac{1}{25}$ of an inch, take a stitch on the edge of the material and return over the same filler, cording it with two more stitches, thus forming a small bar.

SILK POINT—This point was mentioned for the first time in Lessons Nos. 24 and 25.

Carry the hoops forward and backward, but do not turn them. The stitches must always be two forward and one backward. Beginning with the upper part of the design the first stitch must be about $\frac{1}{5}$ of an inch, proceed to the edge, taking two stitches and return with another stitch which may be shorter or longer, according to the variation in color and in design.

SPIRIT POINT—Mentioned for the first time in Lesson No. 29.

Cut out the material and divide the circle into four equal parts. Begin by taking a line of stitching from one of the points which has been marked until reaching the next; there, fasten the thread, turn the hoops and return over the line of stitching already taken, cording $\frac{1}{25}$ of an inch; from that point, continue taking a line of stitching as far as the next point on the edge of the circle, fasten a thread and repeat the operation until reaching the starting point where the lines of stitching should be joined. These lines of stitching are finished by cording them with a double strand of thread from the machine, being careful, in making the points where they are joined together, that the diamond inside the circle is correctly formed. The little loops are made in the usual manner.

HALF STITCH—Refer to Lesson No. 33.

Cut out the material little by little as you proceed with the work; run lines of stitching parallel with each other, endeavoring that they all keep the same distance between each other which should be $\frac{1}{25}$ of an inch; then make lines of running stitches in an opposite direction, taking one stitch between each thread. After the squares have been completed run lines of stitching in a diagonal direction, not starting from the corners of the squares, but a little further down from the sides of the squares, always preserving complete uniformity.

BONE LACE HALF STITCH—Was mentioned for the first time in Lesson No. 33 and this is but another name to distinguish the "Half Stitch".

ENGLISH LACE POINT—See Lesson No. 36 and Lessons Nos. 37 and 38.

SPANISH POINT (LACE)—See Lessons 55 and 56.

CROSS POINT—See Lesson No. 65.

GRANITE OR ROUND STITCH—See Lesson No. 72.

CROCHET LACE POINT—See Lesson No. 93.

Names and Expressions of Common Usage

CORDING—This was mentioned for the first time in Lesson No. 2.

Cording consists in covering guides of several classes and sizes with stitches taken from left to right and vice versa, moving the hoops parallel with the length of the machine as per instructions contained in Rule No. 2. The stitches must be very close together but taking care that they are not superimposed and not to pierce the thread with the needle.

EYELETS—Were mentioned for the first time in Lesson No. 3.

Take a line of stitching over the outline, cut the upper thread, raise the presser bar lifter and draw a strand of thread to reinforce the line of ordinary stitching already taken. In making this reinforcement the stitches are to be taken from right to left, leaving a little space between each. Cut out the material from the interior of each eyelet and cord the edge with a double strand of darning cotton. At the joining point cut the filler and take 3 or 4 stitches to properly secure the threads. If the eyelet is small, a stiletto should be used to pierce the material instead of cutting it out, so that all the eyelets may be of the same size as the design, and then cord as explained.

CIRCULAR DARNING—Was first mentioned in Lesson No. 4.

Take one stitch after another between each of the lines of stitching which form the crossing. They must be taken as near the center as possible and going over the surface as many times as the size of the darning may require.

SMALL BARS—Mentioned for the first time in Lesson No. 5.

Cut out sufficient material from the interior of the design to make a bar and take a line of running stitches from one edge to the other at the rate of 16 stitches per half inch, in accordance with the table. Turn the hoops and take another line of running stitches until reaching the starting point. Then raise the presser bar lifter and carefully draw off sufficient thread from the needle to use as a filler and cord the lines of stitching already taken.

SPOTS—These were referred to for the first time in Lesson No. 8.

When they are large a strand of darning cotton is to be basted around the outline and then the spot is to be filled in with long stitches, which are taken first in one direction and then in an opposite direction. Finish by making raised embroidery stitch in the same direction with that of the first filling stitches. The small spots are made by covering the space from edge to edge with long stitches and then making the raised embroidery in an opposite direction.

STITCHES ON THE BIAS—Were mentioned for the first time in Lessons Nos. 10 and 11.

These are taken in an oblique direction. For the raised embroidery, in making the stems, these stitches must be taken from one edge to the other, the same as for simple cording. In making shaded embroidery they are made in the same manner as the so-called silk stitch.

SIMPLE ZIG-ZAG—Referred to for the first time in Lesson No. 13.

Take a line of running stitches in a broken line, draw a strand of thread from the machine, cord the stitching until reaching the edge, turn the hoops and continue cording the next section of the broken line until reaching the opposite edge, fastening it at a distance of $\frac{1}{25}$ of an inch from the edge and so on until the entire zig-zag line has been completed.

DOUBLE ZIG-ZAG—(Intertwined)—This was referred to for the first time in Lesson No. 13.

It consists in two lines of simple zig-zag crossing each other at opposite angles, that is to say, the lines running in a direction opposite to each other.

CORDED LOOPS—Were mentioned for the first time in Lesson No. 17.

When the bars have loops, a double or buttonhole stitch is made up to about half way the length of the bar. There the thread is corded in a length of about ⅕ of an inch, and holding it in the center with a crochet needle or the points of scissors, the thread is folded and the two ends are joined with a stitch at the same place where the double or buttonhole stitch was interrupted, and then continue with the latter.

BONE LACE LOOSE LEAVES—They were referred to for the first time in Lesson No. 17.

Take a line of running stitching of the same length as the leaf that is to be made. This line will serve as the vein of the leaf. Then take a strand of darning cotton of the length required and fasten it at the point where the line of running stitching ends, and fasten it at about half way the length of the strand so as to have two filler threads, which are corded together with lines of stitches taken up to a distance of ¹⁄₂₅ of an inch from the edge. At that point separate the threads, one remaining on each side of the line of stitching. Then make the darning, taking one stitch outside of the left thread, another between the left thread and the line of stitching; a third on the right of the line of stitching, and finally a stitch on the outside of the right thread. Continue towards the opposite side and vice versa, gradually separating the threads until reaching half way the length of the leaf, that is to say, its widest part. Then gradually diminish the width of the leaf until finishing as in the upper edge, being careful not to pierce the threads and to have the stitches very close together.

BUTTONHOLE BARS—These were referred to for the first time in Lessons Nos. 19 and 20.

Take as many lines of stitching as may be necessary according to the thickness that you wish to give to the bar. Then draw a double strand of thread from the machine to serve as a filler and make a buttonhole stitch.

DOUBLE STITCH BARS—These were mentioned for the first time in Lessons Nos. 22 and 23.

These bars are made in the same manner as those with buttonhole stitch, except that the filling must be as thick as the lines of stitching made.

NOTE: The thickness of any bar must always be in proportion with that of the material and should always be somewhat thinner than the edges of the work.

SIMPLE LOOPS—These were mentioned for the first time in Lesson No. 29.

They are used as a finishing touch in connection with cording and are made when an Irish thread filler is used, consequently should not be reinforced. In all other respects their execution is the same as that of corded loops.

TAPERING BARS—These were first mentioned in Lesson No. 29.

There are two kinds, one which is made without a filler and the other with a filler. For the first take a line of stitching on the lace work of the length intended for the bar and return, cording it with as many superimposed stitches as may be required to give it the proper shape, that is to say, they should taper at the ends. The second is made in the same way with the exception that when cording the line of stitching, a strand of thread from the machine has to be used as a filler. This method is used when making large and heavy bars.

DIAMOND—Was mentioned for the first time in Lesson No. 29.

This is another name by which the "Spirit Point" is known.

PICOT EDGING—This was first referred to in Lesson No. 16.

There are two kinds of picot edging used with corded bars; the first is made by cording the bar up to the point where the picot is to be made and crossing the bar horizontally with a strand of thread, which is held with both hands and cording $1/12$ of an inch on each side, and then cutting the surplus ends of the thread. This is finished by cording the bar. For the second variety of picot, cord the bar to the point where the picot is to be made, take a strand of thread and place it parallel with the bar at a distance of ¹⁄₂₅ of an inch, take one stitch, enclosing the strand and return over the same, cording it with two or three stitches until getting back to the starting point, then pull the strand and the picot will remain loose. Afterwards continue cording the bar.